Small
Business
Marketing
In A Week

John Sealey

John Sealey is a marketing authority, international speaker, author and marketing coach. He helps businesses attract and keep customers, more profitably, with the least amount of effort. John works to show that an enterprise can thrive using proven marketing ideas to achieve more sales and profits. What he uses in his own business and teaches other business owners isn't just theory, but strategies and tactics that work in the real world.

Teach® Yourself

Small Business Marketing In A Week

John Sealey

First published in Great Britain in 2013 by Hodder Education

This edition published in 2016 by John Murray Learning

Copyright © John Sealey 2013, 2016

The right of John Sealey to be identified as the Author of the Work has been asserted by him in accordance with the Copyright, Designs and Patents Act 1988.

Database right Hodder & Stoughton (makers)

The *Teach Yourself* name is a registered trademark of Hachette UK.

British Library Cataloguing in Publication Data: a catalogue record for this title is available from the British Library.

ISBN 9781473609334

eISBN 9781444184068

1

The publisher has used its best endeavours to ensure that any website addresses referred to in this book are correct and active at the time of going to press. However, the publisher and the author have no responsibility for the websites and can make no guarantee that a site will remain live or that the content will remain relevant, decent or appropriate.

The publisher has made every effort to mark as such all words which it believes to be trademarks. The publisher should also like to make it clear that the presence of a word in the book, whether marked or unmarked, in no way affects its legal status as a trademark.

Every reasonable effort has been made by the publisher to trace the copyright holders of material in this book. Any errors or omissions should be notified in writing to the publisher, who will endeavour to rectify the situation for any reprints and future editions.

Typeset by Cenveo® Publisher Services.

Printed and bound in Great Britain by CPI Group (UK) Ltd., Croydon, CR0 4YY.

John Murray Learning policy is to use papers that are natural, renewable and recyclable products and made from wood grown in sustainable forests. The logging and manufacturing processes are expected to conform to the environmental regulations of the country of origin.

Carmelite House
50 Victoria Embankment
London EC4 0DZ
www.hodder.co.uk

Contents

Introduction   2

Sunday   4
    Preparing the ground

Monday   16
    Sowing the seeds

Tuesday   34
    Cultivating your crop

Wednesday   50
    Harvesting your crop

Thursday   70
    Harvesting your crop (continued)

Friday   86
    Growing new crops

Saturday   106
    Knowing how much your crops will yield

7 × 7   118

Answers to questions   124

Introduction

It's been said that the most important area for any business to focus on is its marketing. Of course, there are areas like finance, customer service, and the product or service itself which are key, but without good marketing approaches, there's no revenue for your account systems to do their job, there's no customer to serve and the product or service becomes redundant.

Most business owners are experts in what they do and so they should be. What they also have to be good at is marketing what they do. And if you feel there's more you could be doing on the marketing front, then this book will give you those ideas.

As a small business owner you get involved in all aspects of your business and marketing is such a large field, you can't be expected to learn everything you need in one day. So to break down this behemoth of a topic, we'll approach it a bite at a time.

You have in your hands a tool that will guide you through what's needed day by day over the period of a week. That way you're not trying to eat the elephant all at once. The unpredictable nature of marketing your business will start to disappear, as I walk you through the necessary steps needed to make your marketing efforts more effective than ever before.

Some of the ideas you may already be implementing, while others may well be new to you. Either way, putting them together into a proven system will enable you and your business to thrive, regardless of the economic climate you find yourself in.

If you look closely at the chapter titles for each day, you'll notice they resemble a process of an age-old endeavour. It's the endeavour of farming.

Sit back and think about how a farmer reaps a bumper harvest. He starts off by preparing the land. Once the land has been prepared, he begins to plant the seeds needed. To achieve a harvest which will reward him, he has to cultivate the crop. Once the crop is ready, he harvests it, takes it to market and realizes its value.

And then it starts all over again.

Your business runs in a similar way. You have to ensure that you've planned and prepared for your success, that you're using marketing strategies to attract customers, that the nurturing you do improves conversions (turning prospective customers into actual ones), and that the marketing methods you use increase sales and profits.

You're about to learn, in a week, how you can have a marketing system that enables you to attract, win and keep more customers and, as a result, build your sales and your profitability.

SUNDAY

Preparing
the ground

For any business to be successful there has to be an element of planning and preparation. There are principles that need to be clearly identified which will enable you to get a picture of where your business is currently, and what needs to be done to ensure that you have prepared solid foundations.

Having a good foundation in place is important. In a building, the deeper the foundation, the more likely the structure will be to withstand the elements. In the case of a business, it's better positioned to survive and thrive.

Today is more about understanding what makes your business different, your customer and the positioning of your offering.

Go through today with your mind open and questioning what you've been doing to date. By doing that, you'll be shoring up your foundations and giving your market a clear indication of why they should be using you.

What is your business and why are you in it?

The first part of this question is pretty obvious. What is your business?

Your first lesson is to understand this: you're not in the business you're in, you're in the business of benefits. Listen to other business people's responses to 'What business are you in?'

You'll hear such things as, I'm:

- an accountant
- a plumber
- a lab technician
- a builder
- a business consultant
- a motor dealer
- a window cleaner
- a supply chain manager

And the list goes on.

What people are really asking is, 'What is it that you do which could help me?' They're asking for solutions to problems, not what the business is.

It's very easy to say 'I'm in retail' or 'I have an art gallery'. But it's much harder to say what being a retailer or curator of an art gallery delivers in the way of benefits.

So the first thing to explore is: 'What business are you in?'

If you think about it, printers are not just printers, they're actually in the communications business. They can help others communicate whatever they want to, in a way that produces the desired result. And a good printer will use their knowledge, gained from past experiences, to advise their customers on the best way to do the job.

So whenever a printer is asked 'What is it that you do?', the reply should be along the lines of: 'I help people determine the best path to achieving their desired result using different forms of printed communications'.

That's a benefit-oriented answer to a standard question. It's an answer that will enable this printer to stand out from all the rest. It's also an answer which makes it difficult for people to pigeonhole our printer. And who likes to be pigeonholed?

You're not in the business you're in, you're in the business of benefits.

The future success of your business

Think about where you see your business in two to five years from now. As planning goes, it's a good exercise. As the saying goes, 'If you don't know where you're going all roads lead there'. So, if you know what you want your business to look like a few years from now, and why it's important that your business is successful, you'll be on your way to putting in place the things which will help you get there.

One of those things is what you stand for; more to the point, what values you want your business to uphold. It'll be these values which distinguish your business from others in your industry. These values will guide you in the direction of the ideal customer for your business.

You'll now start to identify your target market. Being clear about who your customers are will make other areas of your planning easier.

With every market there is competition. As part of your planning and preparation you need to identify the competition and, more to the point, who your major competitors are.

Being able to separate yourself from your competitors will be important in the battle to dominate your market and in enabling your marketing efforts to be successful.

Look at customers' feedback to see what competitors do well and what they don't do so well. Check the forums that your target market may frequent and visit sites where customers may leave reviews. Search the places where you can get information on how well, or how badly, your competitors are doing.

This information will be part of your plan to separate you from the rest. By articulating what your competitors do compared to what you can do, you're beginning to show the market how your business is different from theirs.

Articulating your difference

You now have the beginnings of a 'USP', better known as a 'Unique Selling Proposition'. Being able to state your uniqueness in all your communications will give you a big advantage.

Work through all the ways in which you can communicate your USP. For example, via your:

● flyers
● website
● business cards
● mailers
● invoices
● signage
● counter receipts
● commercial logo (or radio jingle if you advertise on radio)
● sales presentations
● networking events.

You get the idea. Your USP needs to be incorporated into everything you do. As part of today's task I'd like you to sit down and map out where your USP could be used. Think of all the different communications you use and aim to add your USP statement to each.

So, whenever people think of your product or service, your USP springs to mind and gives them an instant reason to deal with you. For example, when people think 'credit card' globally, they may well remember the American Express slogan 'Don't Leave Home Without It'. That USP statement is recognized worldwide.

You may not want to dominate the world, but you can dominate your local market with a good USP.

Lifetime value in your planning

If you want to dominate your market, you need to ascertain how much a customer is worth to you over their lifetime. Why is this important?

Because you can then make important decisions on how much you're prepared to spend to win them in the first place.

Let's say, for example, a business works out that the average period of time a customer will continue to buy from them is five years, and that over this period the amount they will spend is £10,000. This is commonly known as 'Lifetime Value'. That business may decide they are willing to lose a small amount upfront, or break even on the first transaction, in order to win that customer, knowing that if they keep them over the average lifetime, there is £10,000 on the table.

In marketing terms this is called 'Acquisition Allowable', i.e. how much you'll allow yourself to win a new customer.

You may have different categories of customer. Some will be worth more than others. So part of your planning will be to categorize your customers and attribute an allowable cost to each. Calculate the lifetime value of each category of customer and how much you're prepared to spend on them.

Your key message

A number of businesses aren't well positioned in the minds of their market, but having a key message in your marketing communications will help you to achieve this.

Thinking about what you'd want your key message to be is an important step in the planning process. The work you've done so far on establishing what your competitors do, and don't do, can be the beginnings of creating a good clear message that would resonate with your market.

A clearly stated message will help you stand out and be noticed by those who might purchase what you offer. You can be squarely positioned as the natural choice for customers once you know what your key message is and have articulated it. Will your message be customer-centred, or product- or service-centred?

To start, grab a piece of paper and write down your answers to the following questions:

1 What market do you want? or What market are you serving now?
2 What fears, problems or frustrations are associated with this market?
3 What solutions are available?

4 What proof do you have that what you offer provides a comprehensive solution?
5 How different are you from others?

Your answers will form the basis of your key marketing message, i.e. the key thing that will have your market feeling that you understand them.

What others say about you

As you're finding out today, there are many ways to prepare your ground, and these will determine how well you're prepared for success.

Knowing what others say about you, or what you want others to say about you, can be the basis of a very good plan. It will guide you towards the sort of marketing tactics you'll be putting to work.

Answer the following questions to decide what sort of marketing approaches you should be using:

1 What would you like your customers to say about your business?
2 What would you like your suppliers to say about your business?
3 What would you like your competitors to say about your business?
4 What would you like the local community to say about your business?

By answering these questions, you're setting out your stall to deliver what your customers want. If you identify what you want customers to say about your business, you'll create a business that delivers just that. The same can be said for suppliers, competitors and the local community. You are planning a business model for success.

Buying activity

You'll need to measure how well your marketing initiatives are working. We'll go into more detail on this on Saturday but, for now, all you need to know is that you'll need systems to track your efforts. Whatever you're offering to your customers, you should know how much the average customer buys. And, as part of your monitoring, you'll be able to see instantly whether customers are falling below this figure or increasing; either way it tells you something.

If they're falling, it's an early warning system for you. Are they buying from someone else? Are they unhappy with you for some reason which has resulted in the lack of orders? Is their business in trouble? Could you help them by providing better terms, or should you be considering getting in money now from outstanding invoices?

On the other hand, perhaps they are winning new customers and thus increasing their buying frequency. Can you cope with their new requirements? If not, will they go elsewhere? What plans should you put in place to meet their increasing demand and enable you to continue to serve them?

Keeping an eye on your customers' buying activities can give you a lot of information, which can either earn you more sales and profits, or save you from losing money.

Each customer will have an average number of orders or purchases. Knowing what this is puts you in a position to pre-empt their needs and position your business positively.

Supporting your customers

What if your business develops quickly? Will you be able to support your customers? There is nothing worse than putting out a message of good customer service, great products or superb services, only to let your customer down because you can't deliver.

If the word gets around that you don't deliver on your promises, then you'll lose business very quickly. The hard work and effort you've put in will count for little.

Your planning should take into account this 'What If' scenario. You'll need to plan for growth, so you don't jeopardize any future business with your existing customers.

Summary

Your challenge here is to ensure you that you're planning and preparing your ground properly. Failing to take this fundamental step will lessen the impact your marketing will have in the future. Foundations for any endeavour are important, especially with marketing.

Having a clear idea of where your business will be in a few years from now can not only drive you but also help you to identify the marketing approaches you need in order to reach your goal.

Every business is different but not everyone knows how to articulate that difference so customers know why they should buy from you. It's important to differentiate your business from the rest so that yours stands out.

Knowing the lifetime value of your customers gives you an indication of how your business should be set out, along with what measurements system you should have in place to ensure that what you do works or to allow you to make changes if it isn't working.

The message you communicate to the market will determine your positioning, so be clear what message you want to share. Others will talk about you, and you have an opportunity to influence what they say through your key message and by delivering on your promises.

It's all well and good having great marketing communications, but you need to keep an eye on how often your customers are buying and support them as your business grows.

Fact-check (answers at the back)

1. **What does a business need to do to be successful?**
   a) Pick a location with parking ❑
   b) Ensure they inform the local authorities ❑
   c) Plan and prepare ❑
   d) Have at least one customer to start with ❑

2. **What should you say, when asked, 'What business are you in'?**
   a) Say you're in the X business ❑
   b) Tell people you sell Y products or deliver Z service ❑
   c) Share the fact that you're a small business owner ❑
   d) Share with them the outcomes and benefits you deliver through your business ❑

3. **How would you find out about your target market?**
   a) Ask the person living next door ❑
   b) Visit forums where your market hangs out ❑
   c) Leave flyers out for all and sundry to call you ❑
   d) Ask a policeman ❑

4. **Why is it important to differentiate yourself from others?**
   a) To enable your business to stand out and to share your uniqueness ❑
   b) It's not vital to stand out. ❑
   c) So people can see you're in business ❑
   d) So people know where you're located ❑

5. **Why is it important to know the lifetime value of a customer?**
   a) So you know how much bonus you can pay your sales staff next month ❑
   b) So you know how much to invest to win a customer ❑
   c) There's no need to work out a lifetime value ❑
   d) Because it helps to determine market share ❑

6. **Having a measurement system in place for your marketing helps you to:**
   a) Determine which customers should get an invoice that day ❑
   b) Share with your friends how well you're doing ❑
   c) Decide who to partner up with in the future ❑
   d) Measure how well your marketing is working ❑

7. **A key message will:**
   a) Help you stand out and be noticed, if it's articulated clearly ❑
   b) Give your customer details of a specific offer ❑
   c) Tell your customers not to buy from competitors ❑
   d) Let customers know what time you open ❑

8. **What others say about your business isn't important:**
   a) Yes that's true ❑
   b) No, it's the opposite ❑
   c) Maybe ❑
   d) Only when you win an award ❑

9. How does knowing a customer's buying activity help you?
a) You know how much to overcharge them ❏
b) You know how many shares you should invest with them ❏
c) It gives you an early warning system for any increase or fall in sales ❏
d) It's just being nosey ❏

10. You should support your customers if:
a) Your business develops quickly ❏
b) Their house is on the line ❏
c) There's no need to support them, refer them to the competition ❏
d) It just makes life easy for you ❏

MONDAY

Sowing
the seeds

Yesterday you went through the steps to preparing your ground. But to get the returns you want by attracting the right type of customer, you need to be sowing the right seeds. Focusing on your target market with tailored messages delivered in a way that the customer understands, will bring you a wealth of interest.

Today we'll examine what else you can do, if you're not doing some of these already, to enable you to bring in more customers and more sales.

You can think of 'sowing the seeds' as the marketing tactics you employ to attract prospects. Some businesses use more tactics than others. The key thing is to have approaches which you've tested and measured to ensure that they're effective and worth using.

Your existing acquisition strategies

You may have been running your business for a while and have marketing strategies in place already. How well are they working for you?

You need to know how well (or otherwise) your existing strategies are working, so you can decide whether to drop them if they are not working and costing you money, or whether to increase their use if they're pulling in responses.

In addition, now you've gone through Sunday's planning, are your existing strategies right for the target market you're after?

Knowing what works and what doesn't will enable you to make decisions about what you do with your existing marketing strategies.

Your marketing objectives

Whenever you put out a marketing communication, it should have an objective. Many would say, of course, the objective is to make more sales and increase profits. And they would be right, but that's the ultimate goal, and there are steps which will lead to that eventually.

You need to know what you want to accomplish through your marketing activities. Let's say, for example, that your marketing objective is to have your market regard you as a trustworthy business and a 'safe pair of hands'.

Now the objective of your marketing communications will share messages which highlight these attributes. If you have different categories of customers, you may need different marketing objectives for each. There will be various considerations when determining your objectives.

When you know your target market well, and have categorized the wants and needs of each group of customers (if you have different groups), you can tailor your marketing messages and communicate with your customers in a way they understand and will get excited about.

You should also focus on what different methods of marketing you should employ in order to fulfil your objective. You need to be able to measure all of your marketing objectives to see whether you're achieving them. For example, if your objective is to be seen as the market's first choice, whenever they think about buying, you could independently survey customers and prospective customers about businesses in your sector. If the results prove favourable to your business, then your marketing objective has been met.

Your marketing communications

Effective headlines

The headline on your marketing piece pulls in the reader and takes them onto the next part of your communication. So it's the most important part of your message. This applies to your website, sales letters, brochures, flyers, business cards, radio adverts or anything else you use to communicate. Do your current marketing communications have effective headlines? Do they have headlines at all?

Imagine reading your favourite Sunday newspaper, packed from front to back with great news. Now imagine that none of the stories have headlines. How will you know what to read? Will you even bother starting the articles to determine what you'll stick with and read?

The answer is probably no.

Now imagine sending your marketing communications with no headlines. Most people are pressed for time, and don't want to be interrupted, so you have to be able to stop them in their tracks long enough to read or to listen to what you have to say. That's the job of your headline.

Your headline should reach out and show the reader that what you're sharing is of interest to them. You can get ideas for your headlines from the research you did in forums and other places, into who your ideal customer is and what's important to them.

Your headline takes your audience by the hand and leads them through to the next stage of your material. You will need to measure how well your headlines work, and revise them accordingly until you have a headline that elicits the best response.

Your offer

Regardless of what you're selling, making an offer of some kind can be incredibly powerful and is worth trying. And it can increase your sales and prospects.

So what constitutes an offer?

The list of what you could call an offer is endless: price reductions, free samples, discount coupons, free information packs, strong guarantees, free seminars, easy payment options... I could go on.

For example, a swimming pool company could offer an extra five feet of pool, at no extra cost, if the customer buys off-season. Your offer can be anything, as long as the customer can see the value in it.

The question is: do you currently include offers in your marketing? And if you do, are they working as well as you expected?

Small business owners try offers, but sometimes they just don't have the sort of impact that they would like. So what can you do to ensure that your offers work better and attract more business?

To begin with, make sure that your offer gets noticed. Don't just tag it on at the end of a communication: sometimes the reader won't get that far, especially if there isn't a compelling headline, and they won't see your offer.

Avoid making your offer in lacklustre communication. No matter how good an offer is, it'll fail if the communication vehicle you're using is weak.

Secondly, there's sometimes little logic to the offer a business makes. So be wary of this and ensure that your offers are relevant to the product or service you're presenting.

Worse still, if not presented in the right way, the offer may come across as a cheap bribe, which puts off the customer. This defeats the object of putting the offer together in the first place. By testing your offers regularly, and measuring the responses you get, you can develop a depth of knowledge about what your customers find relevant and what they don't, what they find attractive and what turns them off.

Finally, the value of the offer should be explicit in your communication. The perceived value should be high. For example, if you were in professional services and you were offering a free information pack, but in your marketing piece you wrote something vague like 'Buy now and receive a free information pack detailing my range of services', your readers would be justified in saying 'Big deal' or 'So what?'

However, repositioning with a skilfully constructed description of the pack could turn the entire communication on its head, in a positive way, and create more sales. For example, you could add the fact that there are Frequently Asked Questions (FAQs) along with, the repositioning element, Should Ask Questions (SAQs). The SAQs will help to position you as a business that really wants to help, as you're sharing questions that should be asked about your type of product or service, which most people don't think of. An additional benefit is that it might attract your ideal customers, who will give you their contact details. In contacting you, what they are actually saying is 'I'm in the market for what you're offering either now or in the future.' This is a way of building a well-targeted prospect list.

Your offers need to be compelling, well-targeted and display great value for money.

Your copywriting

This isn't a book on copywriting; there are plenty of those in bookstores that you can read. But you have to pay attention to how your copy reads.

Your existing copy must be cohesive and flow logically. Here is a checklist for you to use against your existing copy. If you've missed anything, or you feel your copy could be better, use this checklist to improve what you already have.

● Does your communication attract the right audience?
● Does your communication hold the audience?
● Does your copy create desire?
● Do you prove that your product or service is good value for money?
● Do you establish confidence?
● Do you make it easy for prospects to take action?
● Do you give your prospects a reason to take action immediately?
● Do you have a headline, and is it compelling?
● Do you have a guarantee (also known as a risk reversal)?
● Do you explain the advantages and benefits?
● Are 75% of your words fewer than five letters long?
● Are there fewer than five sentences in a paragraph?
● Do you use similes?
● Do you use analogies?

These are just a few of the questions to consider, which can help improve your copy. Many of them can be used in the various communications you have in your existing strategies.

Yesterday, we discussed your key message and how it helps your business. When answering the questions above, think about how your key message can be included in each part of the copy.

Copywriting is a skill every small business should have in its marketing arsenal. And it can be learned with practice. Many business owners find it challenging to write marketing communications. But by using the checklist above, you'll be a long way forward in getting your copy to produce the responses you want.

Prompting people to act

One of the ways to prompt people to act, as I've mentioned is by having an offer and outlining its benefits. You need to take your prospect or customer by the hand and tell them what to do; don't leave it to them to take that next step.

When getting people to act and take the next step, you give them a 'Call To Action' (CTA):

● Phone NOW!
● Call Today!
● Use the code at the bottom of this page now
● Send in your order while stocks last
● Limited time offer
● Everything must go by Wednesday

Your audience need a reason to contact you straightaway. The nature of your business will determine which CTA you use, but you must use one in order to increase the response rates of your communications.

Advantages and benefits

Whether you're presenting your offerings face to face, via email, in a brochure, through a flyer, on your website, or in a specialist report, you need to share what the advantages are and how they benefit the prospect or customer.

Many marketing pieces will go into great detail describing the features of a product, but rarely will they go into the advantages and benefits. On Sunday I talked about your not being in the business you're in, but in the business of benefits. This applies to your copy.

Your prospects or customers aren't so much buying the features of what you're offering, but what it can do for them.

Go through your existing materials and see whether your focus is on the features or whether you have enough advantages and benefits included. If the former, set aside some time to rectify it.

A low cost approach to direct mail

Include a guarantee. I learned a long time ago, when I started writing copy, to always include some kind of guarantee – if you reverse the risk for the reader, they are more likely to say yes to your offer.

One way to make your guarantee effective is to mention it in four separate places throughout your communication. I usually mention my guarantee, or risk reversal as it's also known, at the same time as the offer. I have a guarantee section that has its own subhead and a block of text which is dedicated to it.

With a direct mail piece, it's also a good idea to include an order form. Again, I'd highlight my guarantee there as well. That way, if the order form gets separated from the sales letter, it can do a selling job as a standalone communication.

Additionally, I'd include the guarantee in my PS (post script). The PS is one of the first things which are read in sales letters, even though it's at the end. This is because people are intrigued to see who has sent them the sales letter, and go straight to the end to see the signature. And that's where they see the PS.

Something that many people aren't aware of is the little-known 'Third Headline'. We know about the main headline and subheading, but there is a third.

Remember, the goal of any headline is to get people to read the opening first paragraph, while the objective of a subheading is to get them to continue reading, to provide a little eye relief, and to 'write for those who like to skim'.

The first sentence of each of your paragraphs is called the Third Headline. This sentence persuades the reader to continue reading; at the beginning of each paragraph you want a strong and intriguing opening like:

- Now get this....
- Let's move a bit closer to the truth...
- That's only half the story though...
- Here's a neat little trick...
- What's next?

You get the idea. Each beginning has a few words that will get a reader interested in what comes next. They're called transitions. They give you a chance to tell your magical story.

Keep any direct mail you receive which you find interesting and gets your attention, so you can study and emulate it. Write it out in longhand so you get a feel of what the copywriter was thinking and an idea of their method of writing. This is how a lot of good copywriters learn their craft.

There are many great copywriters both past and present, but one of my favourites is Gary Halbert. Gary was a superb writer and could craft a brilliant sales letter for anything.

This is something you can do with your direct mail, that Gary was a master at. He would open up with some dramatic statement and then translate it in a way which would hit the readers' four biggest sources of frustration. After that, he would go into a list of well-written bullet points, which effectively positioned the benefits of the proposition. Finally, he would present his offer and, of course, provide a guarantee.

In addition, use positive phrases, as many times as you can. There are few writers who can spin a piece of copy with a negative tone and persuade people to buy. Don't fall into the trap of copying other adverts from local businesses who use phrases like 'Don't delay, act today!' You've used the word 'delay' and what are people going to do when you ask them to act? They'll delay.

If you want someone to act, and act quickly, avoid that word. We typically process things only in positive ways. You can put certain suggestions in front of people and they act. If I said 'Don't think of an elephant', what would be the first thing to spring to mind? Yep, an elephant, even though I told you not to think of one.

So, if you say in your communication that this isn't some 'run of the mill, dime-a-dozen product', then you run the risk of the reader thinking exactly the opposite: that it is a run of the mill, dime-a-dozen product.

We all make this type of mistake, but by having a checklist of the key elements in a direct mail (e.g. headline, intriguing opening, including a 'PS', etc.), you can ensure that you have everything covered in your piece.

Press releases

Using press releases has long been a way for companies large and small to get exposure via the media. They can be effective and cost nothing other than the price of a stamp or the press of a computer key to send them via email.

In days gone by, business owners would send targeted press releases to journalists writing for a specific section of a magazine, newspaper or periodical.

However, the way press releases are distributed has changed dramatically; with the arrival of the internet, they can go further and wider, instantly. Although people still write press releases aimed at specialist journalists, writing releases for the media has taken on a new form. Because the web allows you to reach a far wider audience, your press releases need to be created for every potential customer.

You can post press releases to your own website. There are also many press release services, free and paid for, that will distribute your releases across the internet for you. So, far more people get to see what your story is all about. A major advantage of the internet is that, whenever a prospect is searching for words relating to your business, they'll be able to find all sorts of information about you, including your press release.

For example, let's say you sell sausage-making machines, and you write a press release about a new, quicker model you have, which saves customers 50% in time. You post the release on your website and anyone searching for such a machine, using keywords that are also included in your release, will find your website.

They put in an order and buy the machine. All this before any journalist has received your press release; you haven't even distributed it yet. That's an example of how press releases can utilize the power of the internet.

A press release doesn't have to be tied to an event, but you should have something worthwhile to say. You should be getting your press releases out as often as possible, regarding all sorts of things, as long as they're relevant and not thinly disguised adverts. Some rules still apply and this is one of them: whenever you have anything worthwhile to say, put out a press release. It could be about your AGM, your annual report or a new alliance partnership: anything which you feel is legitimate news.

You may have read that you should always include all the 'Ws' in the opening paragraph of your press releases:

● Who
● What
● When
● Where
● Why

If you're only sending press releases to journalists, then this is fine, they want to know quickly whether or not to keep what they have in their hands. But remember, the whole world is your audience and people will spend time reading your release if it's of interest to them.

Here are a few things to bear in mind when writing a press release – some will already be familiar to you:

1 Ensure that your press release pulls people in and gets them interested by asking a question. It's a great copywriting method, which helps to engage the reader. Remember, people are searching on the internet for the type of things you offer, so make sure you include keywords which are relevant. That's how search engines work: they help people find what they want via keywords or key phrases.
2 If you mention a frustration or a problem, ensure you give a potential solution to it, and remember to include advantages and benefits.
3 Everybody likes free advice, suggestions and tips, so include them in your release; people are far more likely to read your release if you're giving away useful information.
4 Avoid writing a release that looks like a thinly disguised advert. That's a sure-fire way for your release to be ignored or deleted.

5 Don't hype up your release or use words which should be reserved for a compelling direct mail piece or an advert. Avoid using jargon.

It's also important to be clear at the outset what you want your press release to achieve. This may sound obvious, but it's essential. If you don't know, it will come across in the release, which may ramble on and end up as a weak piece of communication. So, be clear about your aims, and what you want people to do after they've read the release. If you're writing a press release with your ideal customer in mind, this will determine whether you can answer these questions before you sit down and write.

1 How much do they know about your market/sector/offering already?
2 What's their level of understanding now?
3 Do they need to know or do something before you get them to take action?

Once those questions are answered, you can write a release which is targeted at the right level.

Seeds to sow

The more ways you have to reach your market, the better your chances of attracting the number of customers you would ideally like to have.

What are the existing strategies you have right now? Do you use direct mail and public releases – effectively? Could you do more?

Here is a list of marketing approaches you could add to your existing ones:

email marketing

website

direct mail

flyers

advertising

strategic alliances

host beneficiary relationships

endorsements

sponsorship

TV and radio

using PR

referrals

telemarketing

seminars and special events

trade shows and exhibitions

networking

social media

face-to-face presentations

mobile marketing

cold calling

search engine optimization

search engine marketing

webinars

authorship

tele-seminars

interviews

presenting your own internet radio show

blogging

point of sales materials

signage

text message marketing

Perhaps you're already using many of the above marketing approaches, and some may be working better than others. Your focus should be on the ones that are working well, and making them even more effective by tweaking and testing them. Tweak and test the less effective approaches too, to see if they can be improved.

If your marketing approaches still aren't returning the results you would like, swap them for new ones. You may not immediately get ideal results from the new marketing seeds you plant but, with a little care, thinking about who you're targeting and, of course, making refinements, they may eventually yield the results you're after.

You may also find that it's not always about applying new marketing approaches, but making your existing ones work harder for you.

Summary

Making existing marketing strategies work more effectively for your business is the ideal way to go when sowing new seeds. However, whether you use existing marketing tactics or new ones, you must always have a clear marketing objective.

Your objective will dictate the tone, language and, ultimately, the core message of your communications. There is no point in putting out promotions with no aim; it's akin to saying to a person, who's asking for directions to a specific place, 'Go west'. Yes, they'll go in the general direction, but there's little hope they'll ever get to their destination or, in the case of a business, attract the ideal customer.

Monitoring your sales, the customers you're winning and the level of buying you're receiving, will give you an idea of your ideal customer. Knowing who your preferred type of customer is helps to focus your communications.

Your communications must have a headline of some kind, which will draw the recipient into the rest of your content. Your body copy should include advantages and benefits, to let people know what's in it for them.

Having a strong and compelling offer that adds value is a great way to prompt your audience to take action, so use strong offers as many times as possible.

There are many marketing seeds you can sow; all you have to do today is to work on the ones you want to employ first.

SUNDAY

MONDAY

TUESDAY

WEDNESDAY

THURSDAY

FRIDAY

SATURDAY

Fact-check (answers at the back)

1. Your existing acquisition strategies have no bearing on what new approaches you implement:
   a) That's true, as any new strategy will seamlessly fit in to what is already being done ❏
   b) No, existing strategies do have a bearing on new approaches ❏
   c) Only if the current ones are working ❏
   d) It's not important either way ❏

2. You need to know what you want to accomplish, by having marketing objectives:
   a) This is true as it will keep marketing communications focused and targeted ❏
   b) It might be worthwhile, but it's not vital ❏
   c) I don't need to know that at all ❏
   d) I already know what I want to accomplish, marketing objectives are a luxury ❏

3. Is it a worthwhile exercise to check whether your existing marketing is targeting your ideal customers?
   a) Yes, it is worthwhile, as you get a better return on investment ❏
   b) No ❏
   c) I could check it, but it's too time consuming and not vital ❏
   d) Possibly, however spraying and praying is a better option to catch all customers ❏

4. Having effective headlines in your communications isn't as important as it once was:
   a) True, the world has changed and people now read everything ❏
   b) False. Without a headline, how will people know what's important to read and what isn't? ❏
   c) I don't need headlines ❏
   d) I only use headlines when I'm selling something ❏

5. Having a compelling offer in your marketing can:
   a) Turn people off? ❏
   b) Attract more sales and prospects? ❏
   c) Alert your competition to what you're doing so they can cut their prices? ❏
   d) Show people that you like discounting? ❏

6. Should your existing sales copy be cohesive and flow logically?
   a) Yes, as this will improve the pulling power of the copy and increase responses ❏
   b) No ❏
   c) Maybe, but it's not vital ❏
   d) As long as the audience get an idea of what is being said, cohesion and flow is optional ❏

7. It's OK to leave out a call to action in your communications:
a) Yes, people will act on the information anyway ❏
b) No, you must have a call to action in your communications to encourage people to act? ❏
c) Yes, it's just not important ❏
d) Yes, as long as you include your contact details, that's fine ❏

8. Is it important to have advantages and benefits in your communications?
a) People need to see what the advantages are and how the product will benefit them ❏
b) No ❏
c) Features are better as customers are only interested in how the product works ❏

9. Is it a good idea to add more marketing strategies to your business?
a) Yes, because if one stops working for any reason you have others which are still generating sales and profits for you ❏
b) No ❏
c) You only need one or two, because you don't want to confuse yourself ❏
d) Only if you start getting bored with the ones you already have ❏

10. What's the best way to pull people into your press release?
a) Trying to sell to them? ❏
b) Talking about yourself endlessly? ❏
c) Making your press release look like an advert? ❏
d) By asking them a question? ❏

TUESDAY

Cultivating your crop

By now you're clear about the type of seeds, i.e. marketing tactics, that you should be putting to work in your business. But this isn't where it ends.

It's all well and good putting out marketing communications to attract customers to your business, and articulating a core message so they understand why they should buy from you. Now they're interested in what you're offering, you have to keep them interested, so that whenever they are ready to buy you are the natural and first choice. Many businesses fall down at this point. They've done the hard work. They have their USP, they've created their core message and they have all the measurement tools in place to keep an eye on how well things are progressing. But a key area of their marketing, converting prospects into customers and retaining new customers, often receives little attention.

Nurturing and following up

A business may spend time and money getting its promotional material all present and correct, but lack a nurturing system to follow up prospects that are interested, but not totally convinced.

So today we'll explore what you need to do to ensure that you are not letting any of your hard-earned prospects slip through the cracks. Having a nurturing process in place will assist you in keeping your prospects 'warm', educated and informed until they are ready to buy from you.

If not, all that initial interest will count for nothing, and you may have spent the money to attract them to your offering, only to let your competition in with a nurturing process of their own. In effect, you're doing the hard work of promotion while your competitors are mopping up the leads that are generated. So let's look at what you could be doing right now to increase conversions and nurture your prospects so they say 'yes' to you.

Your systems and procedures for conversion

There are businesses which create promotional materials, put them out into the market, and leave the conversions in the lap of the gods.

For your marketing to be cost-effective, you need to have systems and procedures for following up. People may be interested in your product or service, but if they do not receive a follow-up communication these prospects will fall through the cracks. Avoid losing prospects by putting in place a system for contacting them. The system doesn't have to be complicated; it can be as easy as using a series of non-pushy emails, sales letters or phone calls to reinforce the advantages and benefits of your offering.

Furthermore, if these communications also include a call to action, they will increase the number of people who do say 'yes'.

For example, after a prospective customer has expressed an interest, you might have a system where a communication is sent to them every 90 days or less. It's open to debate how often you should contact them. Some businesses believe that if they send out too many follow-ups, prospects will be annoyed and not buy.

But the opposite is true.

We all live very busy lives, and these prospects aren't thinking about you every minute of the day. So, they need reminding on a regular basis and following up does increase the amount of business won. Just because prospects don't say 'yes' at the first time of asking doesn't mean they won't change their minds. Some businesses will stop following up after the first communication; in fact, research has shown that 44% of businesses will give up after the first rejection:

- 22% give up after the second
- 14% give up after the third
- 12% give up after the fourth communication with no sale.

If you take a look at those percentages, they add up to 92%. That's a huge majority of small businesses who won't follow up after at least four times of trying.

However, it was found that of the decision makers in the household, those who can give you the go ahead, 60–85% of them will say 'no' at least five times before they finally say 'yes'.

That suggests that those businesses who have a procedure to go back to prospects at least five times will win the majority of opportunities. Ensure that you have a system in place to gently, meaningfully and professionally, contact prospective customers regularly so that you win their business.

If you have a team of employees in your business, ensure they know the system, so they understand exactly what needs to be done with prospective customers. They should be aware of all the different procedures they can follow. Nothing is left to chance, nothing is left in the lap of the gods and no one will fall through the cracks.

If, after all, your prospects still say 'no', that's fine. You can either remove them from your prospecting list, or move them to another list of contacts to follow up much later in the future, as things do change.

Contacting your prospective customers

Apart from emails, letters and phone calls, how else could you contact prospective customers? There are a number of methods you could put to work when following up. A newsletter, if done correctly, is a wonderful way to follow up with prospects.

Depending on the frequency of the newsletter, you can contact those prospects, who have previously indicated their interest, on a regular basis. If you add them to your newsletter database then this is done automatically. Remember to include a call to action (CTA) in your newsletters.

Face-to-face nurturing is another option and, depending on the number of prospects, can be a really good approach. Despite all the technology we have at our disposal, personal contact still works very well. In your appointments diary, factor in visits to prospects, when you're in their area. What's the worst that could happen? They say no.

You could also employ a social networking approach, by contacting prospective customers via the likes of Twitter, Facebook or LinkedIn. With this method you don't even need to leave the office, but you can still engage with customers effectively.

Another idea is to record some great material on a CD, put your contact details on the label, and use that as a promotional method. The average car journey to work takes 30 minutes, so that's an hour there and back. You could post your CDs to your prospects, with a covering letter suggesting that they listen to it in the car on the way to or from work. You now have a captive audience, a one-on-one situation with your prospect. You have their undivided attention, and this gives you the opportunity to tell your magical story and give them reasons why you should be a business they buy from.

One final thing, which is important so you don't leave following up to chance or to your memory, is to use a calendar to prompt you to send follow ups.

Your communications calendar

In its simplest form, a communications calendar is a diary of when you should be contacting your customers and prospects. If you contact them with some kind of meaningful communication, like industry news, announcements, or an update on your offering, at least every 90 days, it will keep your business in the forefront of their minds. It makes it a little more difficult for them to forget you.

It's also a good way to forecast, as you know from your conversion rates, how many new clients you can expect at any given stage. Additionally, your calendar will tell you and your team what needs to be sent out, and when, and what the likely results will be. So you know the tone and the approach you need to make.

Ideally your calendar will look like a very large grid, with some spaces blank and some filled in. It will be a kaleidoscope of different colours indicating different types of communications being sent.

The calendar will also tell you whether to continue with your follow up or to move the prospect to a 'follow up in the future' database. Additionally, you'll be able to see which prospects are taking longer to convert and you can start asking the question, why?

Again measurement is coming into play here; you need to be able to measure your conversions.

Creating first impressions

The impression you make on your prospects the first time they meet you, regardless of how that comes about, is one very important element of your marketing.

It sets the tone of what your market will expect. If you can set high expectations, and meet them, then you'll be well on your way to gaining loyal customers, who will continue to purchase from you over a long period of time.

You make a promise in your marketing. You give a certain perception to a market of what they'll get when they do business with you, and everything you do must live up to that expectation.

There is nothing worse than telling a prospect one thing and then giving them something different. This is a fast track way to losing credibility with a marketplace and thus sales. So, the manner in which your phones are answered, especially when someone calls you for the first time, is vital.

Your director of first impressions, as I call them, sets the expectation of what callers will receive and how they'll be treated if they become customers of yours. Therefore, it's important to ensure that everyone is trained on how to answer the phone correctly at all times. Also, make sure your phones are answered quickly, don't keep people waiting, otherwise they'll think you just can't be bothered to answer and perceive that you don't care about them.

When customers walk through your front door, give them a warm and friendly greeting, regardless of whether your cat was run over that morning. People will form an instant impression of you, whether you're aware of it or not, and it will stay with them long after they have left your premises. So always keep it positive.

How you interact with other business owners at networking events, what you put in your blog, how you answer questions when interviewed, how you respond when a customer or prospect calls: all of these add to creating a good first impression. Basically, everything you do counts; everything can create an impression of you and your business in the minds of your market.

Nurture your customer creatively. How about the following ideas?

Strategic alliance partnerships

An excellent way to nurture existing customers, and to gain new ones, is a 'strategic alliance partnership'. This is a partnership between two or more non-competing businesses, whose customer bases are similar. They come together to share resources, which improves customer value and increases their own sales and profits.

Many small businesses that have such an arrangement enter into it out of convenience or familiarity. The arrangement is not purposeful or structured, but more loose and haphazard.

To have a successful partnership there needs to be a solid foundation in place. The benefits of having an alliance with another business can be huge. You can be exposed to prospects that you would have not otherwise have reached, and you're seen to be standing side-by-side with a business which has a good reputation, whose resources you can share.

Like any arrangement, when you're working with another business there are areas you have to keep in mind, such as having a basic business plan, having defined objectives for each aspect of the business, the differing cultures between businesses, the chemistry between you and your partners and, most important, drawing up the contract. These areas have to be on top of a foundation. It's this foundation which will determine whether a partnership will be successful over time or not.

When you leave out the foundation element to an alliance, you're leaving yourself open for this marketing approach to fail. There can be conflicts, misunderstandings that can lead to mistrust between partners, and thus a breakdown of the alliance.

To ensure what's needed to start your relationship off on the right footing, these are the foundation steps you need to consider.

Foundation step 1

You need to begin by taking an inward look at your business. What do you ideally want, where do you want to take your business and how would you like it to look, when your work is done. Consult your staff. This is important if you're to select the right alliance partner.

You need to base your alliance strategy upon the larger vision for your business. By assessing what state your business is in right now, you have a shopping list of your competencies and what unique circumstances you are in at the present moment. This will determine whether an alliance with another business makes sense, rather than making lots of changes to your business, that may not be needed.

What you'll need to be very clear on, is to find an alliance partner whose business culture, strength and market perception are good. That stands to reason. Finding one that can support, not hinder your alliance, is a good foundation.

Foundation step 2

Both parties must be clear that this is a partnership. Not a merger, or one business being dominant over another; you are equal partners in this arrangement for mutual benefit. You're both separate entities and you're working together, jointly, in an arrangement which will further both businesses' aspirations.

So there have to be guidelines and agreed objectives.

When communicating with your market, the market must see what's in it for them. The same can be said of an alliance partnership. Once both parties understand what the other is expecting from such an arrangement, the smoother the arrangement will be.

By working together honestly, so that both parties know what the expectations are, what role each will play and who has responsibilities for what, you'll avoid a potential breakdown and any gridlock in the future. All of this must be clarified before you sign any agreement to work together.

In the same way you went about preparing your ground on Sunday, the same principles apply in your strategic alliance partnership. Rather than just focusing on your own business, there are questions which need to be answered jointly: 'What are our goals?', 'Who are we targeting?' and so on.

Sitting down with a partner, or partners, and talking through why the alliance is important to all involved, how decisions will be made and what the process will be when handling conflict, is going to be crucial. It sets the tone for a mutually successful alliance. Furthermore, all parties should agree on what success will look like through the alliance. Once everyone is clear on these points, the negotiations are over and everyone is happy, you're well on the way to having the right foundations in place.

Foundation step 3

Be prepared to be flexible and move the goal posts, so all parties benefit. Even the best-laid plans will need to change on occasion. You may need to adjust and tweak some areas.

However, keep as close as possible to what the partnership agreed. There is a danger that things can run away with people and the original objective can be lost. Having an evaluation process, where you check progress at certain stages, milestones and benchmarks, will keep the partnership on track. Agree to regularly review where you all are and you should be in good shape.

As you go along, ask such questions as:

1 What went well and why did it go so well?
2 Is there anything the partnership should do differently and why?
3 What was learned in the alliance?
4 What changes within each business had to be made for the alliance to work?
5 What additional skills and knowledge were needed, and will the partnership need more of these for the future?
6 Is there a need to adapt policies, systems and procedures to resolve any issues?

The more systems you have in place to check progress, identify challenges and nail down the processes, the less likely you'll encounter issues which will damage your alliance.

There you have it, the foundational steps needed to create a good strategic alliance partnership. This marketing approach will take you a long way towards cultivating your crop and achieving a bumper harvest.

E-commerce to win new customers

Whenever someone receives a telephone call from a business, they feel they're being pressured to buy. Having an online option for prospects and customers lessens the feeling of being pressed into buying something.

When online your prospects can browse at their leisure and take their time when looking for a product or service. You nurture them: they stay with you.

E-commerce is rapidly becoming the tool of choice for customers in many markets. But what is e-commerce?

Simply put, it's buying and selling products and services over the internet: that's it in a nutshell.

You only have to look at Amazon, Ebay, iTunes and many hundreds of other businesses, to see how internet sales are taking off. And this is only the beginning. There are hundreds of thousands of small business owners, whose businesses lend themselves to some kind of e-commerce solution.

Should your business have an offering that could be sold online, then having an e-commerce solution in place can be a very wise idea. And, with mobile devices in virtually every household, people can buy online anytime and anywhere.

Furthermore, with security and privacy concerns being robustly addressed, e-commerce is set to lift off to tremendous heights in the coming years. You need to be in place and positioned well to take advantage of this opportunity.

Summary

You can have all the marketing approaches in the world, to attract new customers and to position your business as a customer's first choice. But if there is no procedure for following up the opportunities that your marketing creates, your sales and profits will suffer.

Don't expect that all your prospects will say yes at the first time of asking, because they won't. You need to have a plan in place to nurture those who won't say yes straightaway. When they have indicated that they are in the market for what you offer, but they haven't made a decision to use you, then following them up will be critical to your success.

You should try various methods of following up, as prospects have preferred ways of consuming information, to find the best ways to contact individual prospects.

To keep you on task, a communications calendar should be in place. This will, at a glance, tell you what communications to send, when to send them and how long it's taking you to convert prospects into clients. You now have a mechanism that will

SUNDAY
MONDAY
TUESDAY
WEDNESDAY
THURSDAY
FRIDAY
SATURDAY

enable you to make informed decisions about whether or not to continue to follow up certain prospects.

Following up is a vital part of your sales process; it's cultivating your crop, and bringing it to maturity. So, too, is finding creative ways to nurture your prospects and offer them options which will work for them and for you. Or, in other words, winning a 'yes'.

Fact-check (answers at the back)

1. What impact does nurturing and following up customers have?
   a) None at all ❏
   b) It has some impact, but not enough to focus time and effort on it ❏
   c) It increases sales and profits, as you avoid losing customers and you don't waste opportunities. ❏
   d) It's hit and miss, so has a limited impact ❏

2. Why is it important to have systems and procedures for conversion?
   a) It helps to prevent losing prospects, and will streamline your marketing functions ❏
   b) Your business will be in line with other similar business types ❏
   c) Your accountant will love you for it ❏
   d) It's not important at all ❏

3. Should you contact your prospective customers?
   a) No ❏
   b) Yes if you want to annoy them ❏
   c) Yes, keep in contact with them so you can nurture, educate and inform them so that when they are ready to buy they think of you ❏
   d) Only on an ad hoc basis when you remember ❏

4. Communications calendars should be used mainly because:
   a) They're a memory aid for you ❏
   b) They help you to keep track of your mailings and how far along prospects or customers are in the sales process ❏
   c) Not sure why but it sounds like the right thing to do ❏
   d) You shouldn't really use them ❏

5. In a strategic alliance partnership, which of the following should both parties bear in mind?
   a) That this is a merger ❏
   b) That their company is the dominant one ❏
   c) That both companies are equal partners, in the arrangement for mutual benefit ❏
   d) That each company should focus on its own goals, and not share its aspirations with the other partner ❏

6. A major benefit of a strategic alliance partnership is:
   a) It's convenient ❏
   b) You don't have to make any effort ❏
   c) It helps you to nurture existing customers, and to gain new ones ❏
   d) You can steal a competing company's customers ❏

7. How do you create the right first impression with visitors?
a) It's more important to answer the phone quickly than to pay attention to how you greet people ❏
b) Don't be too concerned about what people think when they visit your business, it's the marketing that's important ❏
c) Everything counts when it comes to creating a good first impression. People will access your business through different channels, so you need to be consistent. ❏
d) Throw a few ideas together and hope they do the job ❏

8. After a prospective customer has indicated an interest in your offering, how often should you follow up if they don't buy straightaway?
a) Once every six months? ❏
b) Annually? ❏
c) Every 90 days or less? ❏
d) If they don't buy at the first time of asking, give up? ❏

9. Research has shown that 60–85% of decision makers say 'no' to an offering at least how many times before saying 'yes'?
a) five times? ❏
b) four times? ❏
c) three times? ❏
d) two times? ❏

10. A communications calendar can show you:
a) The birthdays of your prospects? ❏
b) Which prospects are taking longer to convert, so you can investigate why? ❏
c) When to contact your suppliers for stock? ❏
d) When to call your accountant for completing your tax return? ❏

SUNDAY

MONDAY

TUESDAY

WEDNESDAY

THURSDAY

FRIDAY

SATURDAY

WEDNESDAY

Harvesting your crop

We've already covered the importance of creating good communications that attract customers and having a nurturing process to win them, if they don't say yes the first time of asking.

What happens when they do finally say yes and buy from you?

If you were a farmer harvesting the crop, you'd have taken time and effort to get to this point. Having won your customers, how do you start to turn them into loyal customers who will buy from you on a regular basis? What marketing skills can you put to work in your business to maximize your sales and profits? Customers' requirements can change, and if a business isn't in constant contact with their customers, they'll miss the opportunity to learn about changing trends and beat the competition.

Upselling and cross-selling to your customers

Upselling

Let's say you walk into an electrical retailer. A salesperson walks up to you and asks 'Can I help you?' Now before I go on, I'd like to add, if you have a team of people on the sales floor, you ensure that question is NEVER asked. The reason?

What's the universal answer? The customer will say, 'No I'm just looking'. Where does a salesperson go from there? All they can say is either 'OK' and walk off, which in my experience many do or 'OK, well if you need any help I'll be over there'. Then they proceed to watch the customer like a hawk and make them uncomfortable. Worse still, they really do walk off and pay no attention when the customer needs help.

A question that salespeople should ask when a customer walks through the door is 'Hello, what advert brought you in today?' Can the customer answer with 'No I'm just looking?' No, they have to engage your salespeople in conversation. Even if they didn't come in as a result of an advert what, subliminally, does that question suggest? That you're proactive in the market, and that you're busy. Therefore, the customer feels they may be in the right place.

Back to the electrical store, a salesperson walks up to you and says, as they have been trained, 'What advert brought you in today?' You go on to say that you're looking for a washing machine.

The salesperson then asks the usual probing questions to get an idea of what exactly you want: size, price, make, model, capacity, etc.

Once they've got a measure of what you're looking for, they then ask a more personal question about the size of your family.

Why ask that question? The salesperson is looking for an opportunity to upsell.

When you say you have a young, growing family, you are shown a washing machine which is a little more than you were prepared to spend. Moreover, you're not sure you can even afford it.

However, when the advantages and benefits of the washing machine are explained to you: it will last longer and be more cost-effective as you won't need a new one while your family are at home, you'll be able to wash more clothes at one time, and so on, you begin to see the reasons for paying that little bit extra. The washing machine begins to look more attractive than the cheaper, smaller version, and you're thinking emotionally about the purchase. The salesperson has upsold to you. Plus, the icing on the cake is that it's on offer right now; to add the extra spice of urgency to the offer, you are told there are only a limited number left. SOLD!

If that wasn't enough, you are persuaded to take an 'easy pay' option so it doesn't affect your bank balance with one lump sum coming out. Double SOLD!

Cross-selling

Let stay with our well-trained salesperson. As you are completing the purchase, they tell you about the benefits of an additional warranty, and how it covers a replacement machine which you'll get the same day, so you're never left with dirty washing. They also tell you about another low-priced product which increases the life of the machine still further.

That's cross-selling.

Our well-trained salesperson has upsold to you a higher priced product instead of a lower-priced one, and then cross-sold to you associated products and services which complement your purchase.

Use these approaches every single time a customer buys from you, professionally and gently, and profits will increase dramatically. Even if one in three say yes, how much more does that add to the average value of a sale? Look at what you offer and see whether you can cross- and upsell products or services, not in an ad hoc way but in a systematic and consistent way. You'll be pleasantly surprised how much it adds to your bottom-line.

This is one way you can start to really bring in your crop and be on your way to achieving a bumper harvest, without having to discount your offering.

Reduce discounting

Discounting is easy to do, but it's very difficult to earn profits if it's done without a strategy in place to leverage opportunities at the back-end (more on this later).

Sometimes small businesses feel compelled to reduce their prices, or discount because their competition is doing it. It's a familiar situation, especially in tough economic times: your competitors reduce their prices and you wonder how on earth they can survive. You could try to push back by reducing your prices, but then you'll find yourself in a price war which nobody wins in the end, not even the customer.

What you have to keep in mind is that there are a variety of reasons why people buy the things they do and at certain prices. If you were a retailer selling sweets and the shop down the road reduced their prices on the same sweets, then customers would go to that shop for the same product. But if your business was cosmetics and your competition were reducing their prices, would it be a good idea to reduce yours? Can you put a price on beauty? People go to a certain establishment for other reasons than price. The value, the expertise, the service: these are the other reasons people will buy besides the price.

In some instances, you could increase your prices and not see a marked fall in sales; in fact, you may actually see an increase. Some businesses aren't charging what they're truly worth, and so there is leeway for them to increase their prices. Some businesses have increased their prices by as much as 30% and no one has batted an eyelid, because they are delivering exceptional value in comparison with the competition. If you deliver on your promises and are good at what you do then people will continue to buy. Furthermore, charge too little, and people will doubt that you can actually deliver.

Is there a danger you'll lose customers by increasing your prices? Yes, of course, but trying to be all things to all people is extremely difficult. If you've made a decision to slash prices, right to the bone, and you're fighting it out with others at the lower end of the market, there are still only a certain number of people who'll buy. And there are others who just won't look at buying a cheap product for one reason or another.

Once you've made a decision where you want to position yourself, then you must fiercely defend that position to the hilt. If you look at your pricing and offerings with a critical eye, you may come to the conclusion that your preference will be to scale up and stay well away from the high volume, price sensitive and narrow margins.

Package products together

All businesses are different and have a multitude of different circumstances. But the idea of packaging products and services together has a universal appeal.

Even if you feel that your business is less than exciting, you can still craft an offer which can position plain-looking products into something a customer will take a second look at. Build a perceived completeness in what you offer, so it becomes unique in the eyes of your customer.

What you're actually doing is separating yourself from others selling the same thing and thus giving your business a differentiating factor. Moreover, you avoid competing on price, which can only be a good thing.

Let me give you an example, and I'm sure this idea will resonate with you. In any fairly sizeable town there are numerous printers, and if there is a sector which survives on price, it's this one. However, if the business is good at what it delivers, then the price issue is far less important. Now the question is, how can a printer package products together to promote how special they are and attract new customers?

Businesses in the town want a printer who really knows what they're doing and can produce brochures, promotional materials and other communications together well.

The printer employs in-house designers and typesetters, who are used to working to short deadlines, have a flair for creative solutions, and can work with a project which has a tight budget. These skills can be promoted as part of a package, along with the printing service.

Offering the different services as a complete package, rather than just a printing job, gives prospective customers a real incentive to use that printer. Rather than going to two or three places to get the job done, it's all delivered under one roof!

That's an example of packaging products or services together to create a powerful proposition. But to present this proposition you have to be in a position to tell your magical story, get prospects to sit and listen long enough and persuade them to buy from you. Selling is a key factor.

Improve your selling techniques

I've been involved in sales for a long time, in many different areas, and I've seen, learned and applied many different selling techniques over the years. But just as I was trained to sell, the people I was selling to learned how to buy.

I was forever honing my skills, approaches and techniques. When you're running a small business you have to do the same. Nothing happens in the way of a transaction, if a sale isn't made, so improving your selling technique is vital.

There are so many different ways to sell, that thousands of books have been published on the topic. Rather than going into specifics, I'll be sharing with you a tool that all sales functions should have: a selling system. You can always wrap specific sales techniques around a system, but a system you must have.

The ultimate aim here is to get you focused on creating your own selling system.

Even if you employ a team of people who are responsible for sales, you know your business better than anyone. So if you were to step up and reach out to customers in a sales situation, would you be the star performer? Would you open more doors? Would you win more face-to-face meetings? Would your conversions be far higher than others who are selling your offering?

The answer to all of these questions is probably yes.

Before you jumped in, the conversion rate was, let's say, two in ten. Now, with your intervention, it has increased to five or even six in ten. How much more could you achieve in sales volume if you could clone yourself, and those duplicates replicated your success?

Far, far more!

It is a crucial question to ask. Businesses everywhere are leaving money on the table for want of a successful selling system that everyone adopts.

Additionally, let's assume that there is one other person who is more successful than the others in your sales team, and you incorporate their skills, as well as your own, into a selling system. How much more would you get in sales?

To create a great selling system for your business you need to inject the skills of the very best people across your whole team.

You will be well on your way to winning more sales, and thus more revenue, if you:

- exploit your own knowledge and expertise to create a selling system that works
- get the involvement of everyone in the sales function.

Your star performer

Firstly, you need to identify who your top performer is and start by finding out what they do that the others don't.

If it's not obvious, then bring them in and ask and, if the opportunity arises, go with them on their appointments, or listen to their calls, and find out for yourself how they make a sale. Note down everything they do, from approaching the prospect to closing the deal.

Look at what they say and do during the appointment or call, how they present your business, what type of questions they ask, and how they invite the prospect to do business with you.

Identify every technique, and this will give you a good start.

Get your team involved

Now it's time to get your team involved and you may hit a bit of a barrier with some of them. They are used to going about their selling in their own way and are comfortable.

At this stage, you need to find a way for those people to contribute to your selling system.

One way of doing this is to get your sales team together and let them know you're doing a survey on conversion rates, because you want to help them in increasing their commissions. That is a powerful incentive for them to buy into this.

After they've given you their feedback you can present the idea of your selling system. Get them involved as you go through it, and by the end of the meeting, they will own it.

Now they have it, it has to be used.

Testing what you have come up with

All that is left is the testing phase. Once your sales team have been trained how to use the system – how it works and what sort of results they should expect – it has to be field-tested.

Get your sales team to use the system for the first few weeks, and then use their feedback to fine-tune, amend and tweak. Go out and do it again.

Try testing different parts of your system one at a time, before you roll out the whole thing. In a matter of months you will have created a system which is powerful in design and successful.

Soft-cost offers

I think the best way to explain what a soft-cost offer is, is to show you how I and other consultants use this particular idea in our own businesses.

I'm always marketing, and the marketing machine is a 24/7 engine. When I have quiet times, I like to fill that time with prospecting for clients in certain niches. Let's say my hourly rate is £200, so if I'm not working, that's how much I'm losing.

I have two options during quiet periods: I can either fritter that time away and do nothing, which is a waste of a valuable resource, or I can 'package it' and harness my down-time as an compelling and valuable offer!

I've shared this idea with other consultants and asked them how many times have they given free advice to a prospect they've been trying to win as a client who, at the end of that free advice, thanked them and just walked away?

So STOP giving away your time and instead value it.

The consulting firm I once worked for actually went as far as writing a cheque for £200, made out to themselves, and mailed it to prospects pinned to the top of an introductory letter saying that the cheque was worth an hour of the company's time.

So, although the value of the cheque was £200, the customer was getting the service for nothing. When you offer something for free, the perceived value isn't that high; however, if you offer something which has a monetary value attached, but you give it away for free, its perceived value is much higher.

Any business can create this type of offer; a gym, for example, may give away free trial coupons. What are they worth? Unless the recipient is shown the real value of what they're getting, it won't be worth anything.

Let's say this savvy gym sends a thoughtfully produced, expensive-looking gift certificate that spells out the services the customers would get, along with the value amount next to each service, and an outline of the programme they'd be on. The gym even goes as far as ringing up the gift certificate on the till when it's redeemed.

Done in the right way, that certificate would attract lots of people, who otherwise may not have entertained the idea of using the gym.

A soft-cost offer can be used in any type of business. Whether you're in retail, manufacturing, wholesale, or whatever sector you're in, soft-cost offers can work just as well. But this marketing approach is just one of many, as you've seen so far, that can help you to harvest sales.

Another approach is to remove any barriers that could prevent a prospect from buying – risk reversal.

Risk-reversal strategy

Being able to remove any hurdle, barrier or doubt preventing a potential customer from buying, can massively increase the number of customers you win and the sales you achieve.

A great way of doing this is reversing the risk for someone buying. And you do that by having some kind of guarantee. Small business owners are very hesitant in using guarantees as a marketing tool, in the false assumption that people will rip them off: they have visions of a hoard of people banging on their door demanding their money back.

Here is the thing: you will win more customers by having a guarantee. You'll be so far ahead in sales that the ones who do ask for their money back will be far outweighed by those that don't.

If you believe in your offering and can stand behind it, there should be no reason why you can't guarantee what you do. Businesses that can't should improve what they do, so they can make guarantees, or seriously think about getting out of that business.

A risk-reversal guarantee is a tremendous marketing tool, as long as you have analysed your business and put right any weak areas. I have previously talked about getting your team to buy into the approaches you promote. This is no different; your team need to know how important it will be to live up to your guarantee. When you think about it, their livelihoods, as well as yours, are linked to any guarantee you promote. By getting your staff involved, they'll feel they are contributing to the success of the business; they'll put forward ideas and be motivated by what you're offering to customers.

Jay Abraham is a world-renowned marketing authority, and he has some wonderful ideas on how to position guarantees. Here are some examples of guarantees you could consider:

The minimal risk reversal

If, in any way, shape or form, your hi-fi develops a fault or defect within 30 days after you arrive home, simply return it and we'll be MORE than happy to replace it on the spot, right there, right then.

'Buy Hi-fi' are SO confident that our hi-fis are made to the highest and very best standard that we're prepared to offer you a no questions, no quibble replacement guarantee. We wouldn't offer such an amazing guarantee if we weren't ABSOLUTELY sure that the hi-fi's we sell weren't the very best manufacturers' from around the world could offer.'

Right up front, even before anyone buys, this guarantee is offering the customer protection, which gives 'Buy Hi-fi' a competitive advantage in the marketplace.

30-Day 100% SATISFACTION GUARANTEE

If you're not 100% satisfied with your new hi-fi, for whatever reason – perhaps the crystal clear sound isn't as promised, the quality of surround sound isn't as expected, or the equalizer isn't performing as it should or, even, that you've simply changed your mind about the colour or the model – return it to us in its original packaging within 30 days and we'll be MORE than happy to exchange it.

In the VERY unlikely event that you don't find the ideal hi-fi, we'll give you a TOTAL, no questions asked, no quibble, no hard feelings refund, right on the spot.

If you re-read this guarantee, what is being said?

It's basically telling the customer that they can return the hi-fi if they're not happy with it, for whatever reason. If someone is in the market for a hi-fi but they're undecided about whether or not they should buy, a major barrier has just been removed with this type of guarantee. All the risks have been eliminated.

This shows the potential customer and the market that the hi-fi company really values their customers. They're prepared to do whatever it takes for customers to be happy. It says 'We want you to walk away completely satisfied and delighted, no matter what it takes. We really value your custom that much.'

Will the customer notice a competitive advantage here over others in the market who are selling hi-fis? Yes, I think they will!

The better-than-risk-free guarantee/risk reversal

100% SATISFACTION GUARANTEED – PLUS VALUABLE FREE GIFT, YOURS TO KEEP

When you purchase your Candle Supreme hi-fi from us, we'll give you 50 top-of-the-range blank rewritable CDs, worth £97.99, ABSOLUTELY free.

In addition to that, if for any reason you're not completely satisfied with the Candle Supreme hi-fi, the crisp sound, the clarity vocals, the fine reproductions of recordings... or if you'd simply prefer a different model or different speakers, return it in its original packaging within 30 days and we will exchange it.

Should you not find what you're looking for we'll give you a full refund on the spot, no questions asked, no quibbles. What's more, if you do decide to return it and receive a refund, you can keep the free CDs as a thank you for your time.

This is such a powerful risk reversal. It's my favourite because it shows the customer that you'll take ALL the risk. They'll make a purchase, which is ENTIRELY risk FREE and, in addition to that, they'll get a free gift for their trouble... simply for trying out the product.

The bounce back offer

You may not have heard of this term, but if I put it another way and call it an 'immediate follow-up sell', would that give you an idea of what this approach is?

Many marketers use this powerful idea and they call it the 'Recency Rule'. The rule says that the most recent customer who buys, is the one most likely to buy again soon after their initial purchase.

In essence, you 'bounce back' with something else that the customer can buy.

Here's an example. Let's say you own a hotel and spa. People enjoy the service, the food is out of this world, as is the spa, and the hotel is in line to win awards for quality, voted for by the guests. The whole experience is fantastic, according to your guests. Have you spotted the opportunity yet?

As guests are leaving, on a wonderful high after their experience, you could offer them a return visit at a quarter of the price, if they come back within three months. You could hand all customers a VIP *Good To See You Again* voucher or coupon. Not everyone will take you up on the offer, but enough may do.

If two out of every ten used the voucher, what would that mean to your business? Without your VIP offer, you would get 100 bookings; with the offer, this has increased to 120 bookings. Can you see an opportunity for a 'Bounce Back' in your own business?

Adding value

There are many approaches to winning new customers when times are tough. But the story I remember best of adding value and winning customers, even in tough times, was from Claude Hopkins, a brilliant marketer in the 1920s.

His ideas and approaches are as relevant today as they were back then.

Claude's company had a client who was number one in the retail market in a certain type of lard, but had real problems cracking the trade side. Claude met with his client and asked them who was the toughest trade company to crack?

The client gave him the details of a company that was really tough and which other companies had just given up trying to win. This company focused on price and were knee-deep in the product Claude was tasked to sell to the trade.

Claude went to see the company and, after just 30 minutes, not only did he walk out with an order, but also with a long-term commitment for a certain number.

How was this achieved?

Instead of trying to sell like many other companies did, Claude created a way to provide a service to this trade customer. After asking the customer questions, to unlock their hidden desires, Claude discovered that their product was sold to 1000 stores.

Straightaway, like a light bulb being switched on, Claude showed the business a new advertising 'street-car card', which was a poster about to be printed. He asked the customer his opinions on it, how he would improve it, thoughts on the colour and other things.

But the customer couldn't see any improvement that could be made. To him it was a perfect picture of the product.

Claude then made the customer an offer, to create a similar card for him, as long as he stated that his product was made with nothing but this particular lard. Claude also offered the customer 250 of the cards for every car load of lard he bought. The customer was chomping at the bit to get his hands on these cards and take the offer. He bought four car loads of lard, so he had enough cards for each of the 1000 stores selling his own product. Can you see where the long term commitment comes in? The customer was locked into buying Claude's lard.

Hopkins used the same 'added value' approach with other trade companies and won big. But the same idea was used in a variety of other industries. Claude Hopkins famously said:

I was selling service. The whole basis of my talk was to help the trade business owner get more business. The advantage to myself was covered up in my efforts to please him. I have always applied that same principle to advertising. I never ask people to buy. I rarely even say that my goods are sold by dealer, I seldom quote a price. The ads all offer service, perhaps a free sample or free package. They sound altruistic. But they get a reading and get action from people seeking to serve themselves. No selfish appeal can do that.

The philosophy of providing a noble service can, more often than not, gain new customers. Claude added value, and the trade customer bought, even though he was knee-deep in the product. The adding value approach is key for you to be able to cross-sell and upsell to more of your customers.

Summary

Once you have a customer there are plenty of opportunities to persuade that customer to purchase more from you. But you have to have systems in place which will do this every single time without fail.

You and your team must harness the power of cross-selling and upselling, to reduce the use of discounting wherever possible (unless it's part of an overall strategy) and to package products and services together, as far as possible.

It's your professional responsibility to ensure that your customer gets everything they can from you when making their purchase, rather than having to go elsewhere for associated items. Make sure a customer has everything they need before they leave. Always look to have your customer buy again soon after they have made a purchase, as this is the time they're more likely to do so. Don't let them make another call or enquiry to another business for a product they could easily get from you. Additionally, sharpen your selling techniques so you and your sales team sell in exactly the same way, using a proven system. This approach alone can push sales and profits skyward.

SUNDAY
MONDAY
TUESDAY
WEDNESDAY
THURSDAY
FRIDAY
SATURDAY

Fact-check (answers at the back)

1. What is 'cross-selling'?
   a) A method of selling associated products and services following an initial purchase ❑
   b) An 'arts and crafts' term for marketing ❑
   c) Reducing the amount customers spend with you ❑
   d) Face-to-face selling ❑

2. When is a good time to discount?
   a) Always discount whenever possible ❑
   b) Only discount when a customer asks ❑
   c) Discount when you have a strategy in place to gain more sales at the back-end ❑
   d) Never discount ❑

3. How effective is packaging products together?
   a) It separates you from the competition and makes your business more attractive to customers ❑
   b) It has no effect at all ❑
   c) It has some effect, but it's negligible ❑
   d) It positions you in the same light as your competitors ❑

4. What is one of the two things you can do to improve your sales technique?
   a) Go with the flow and see what works best ❑
   b) Get outside sales agents to do the selling ❑
   c) Create a selling system that works ❑
   d) There isn't anything which can improve sales techniques ❑

5. What is a 'bounce back offer'?
   a) It's something you offer customers months after their first purchase ❑
   b) It's a weekly discount offer ❑
   c) There's no such thing ❑
   d) It's an offer you put to customers soon after they purchase ❑

6. What was the name of the 1920s advertising and marketing great?
   a) Henry Ford ❑
   b) Howard Hughes ❑
   c) Claude Hopkins ❑
   d) J. Edgar Hoover ❑

7. What's the best approach to testing?
   a) There isn't one ❑
   b) Test one thing at a time ❑
   c) Test everything all at once ❑
   d) Test only once a year ❑

8. What is a 'soft-cost offer'?
   a) When you discount your prices heavily ❑
   b) There's no such thing ❑
   c) A product that is soft to the touch ❑
   d) An offering that has a high perceived value but costs little to deliver ❑

9. What is a 'risk reversal'?
   a) A Health and Safety issue ❑
   b) Another term for a guarantee ❑
   c) Looking at where the risks of doing business are ❑
   d) A way to minimize an investor's exposure ❑

10. Which of the following is a risk reversal?

a) The Total Risk Reversal ❏

b) The Half Nelson Risk Reversal ❏

c) The Dog and Bone Risk Reversal ❏

d) The I'll Do It Tomorrow Risk Reversal ❏

THURSDAY

Harvesting your crop (continued)

Getting a bumper harvest doesn't stop with what we covered yesterday. Your plans should include effective and efficient systems that will drive down wastage, improve the return on your investment and build stronger relationships.

The relationships you build will enable you to attract more and better customers, therefore increasing the value of your sales.

It's important to have a series of marketing approaches in place that can leverage what you have already, so you earn more as a result. The more you have in the way of marketing approaches to attract, win and keep customers, the more profitable your business will be as a result. Implementing the approaches I'm about to share with you will make life a whole lot easier.

Creating the time to plan, and set in place, what you intend to do, gives you more time to work on other areas of your business. With all that said let's look at continuing to harvest your crops.

Welcoming a new customer

You've won a new customer; it's the first time they've used you, so they've made a very important decision and put their trust in you. How do you reinforce that trust in the way you welcome your new customer?

There are very few small businesses that take the time to think about welcoming customers to their business, but yet, it's a very important part of the sales process. The fact that you welcome them, and the way in which you do it, endorses their decision.

Today I'd like you think about the different ways you could welcome your new customers.

Every business is different, of course, and I'll share with you some of the methods I know good small businesses used. This will give you ideas on how you can start welcoming customers to your business. Putting a 'welcome' system in place is part of your retention strategy to help reduce your attrition rate.

What sorts of things can you do in this welcome stage?

- Send a welcome letter.
- Email a welcome message.
- Send a postcard with saying 'Thank you for choosing us'.

In addition, you can use the information you have on the customer to great effect. Yes it's a little more effort, but remember, you're looking to keep this customer for a long time. So, see what I'm about to share as part of your acquisition cost.

I once had a customer in the financial service industry, dealing with clients with a high disposable income, so the average value of a sale for him was very good.

He would learn what his clients' interests and hobbies were and send them relevant gifts. He once told me he had a client who was very interested in West End shows and his children were also keen.

So my customer purchased a set of tickets for his client and his client's children to see a top West End show. He positioned it this way: 'I have these tickets for a show, but it's not really of interest to me; I know you like West End shows so I thought you'd like them instead, as they would only go to waste. If you're free on that evening, they're yours.'

Now how much did they cost?

At the time, they were about £25 each. He spent £75 and was well on the road to having a client for life, building a great relationship, which he still has to this day, and this client became a great referral source for him.

I don't know the total amount of business won as a result of this gesture, but I can safely say it's far more than £75.

Look at the way you welcome customers to your business as a strategic move. The idea is to secure their business now, and into the future, and to have them like and trust you so much they'll be happy to refer others potential customers to you.

Use of the newsletter

This marketing tactic could be made into a book all on its own. It's such an under-utilized marketing approach for many businesses, and those who do use it don't get as much out of it as they could.

In my mind it's one of the most effective, but misunderstood tools for building value and relationships.

Effective, because when you put together a well-crafted newsletter it will inform, educate and entertain your reader.

Misunderstood because, perhaps, only around one in ten newsletters that I've seen does the job intended.

As you go through this section, you'll find there's more to a newsletter than you may have first thought. To make a newsletter work, and work consistently, you need to have a few key elements, which will get your newsletter read and, more importantly, acted upon.

A winning newsletter is well planned, well-constructed and has a long term, positive impact on any business.

This marketing tool builds long-term relationships and it can create a loyal customer base. These are people who are more likely than any other group to respond to your offers, and when you're looking at long-term growth and profits, using a newsletter in this way is a good addition to your marketing strategy. Moreover, these customers are more likely to refer you to others like them.

Your newsletter should be an informative communication tool, which gives you the opportunity to talk to your targeted customer in a way that isn't pushy or giving a hard-sell. Look at it as if you were having a chat with a friend in a social setting: that's the tone you should use.

So, how do you get your newsletter right? How do you avoid the pitfalls and traps that many small businesses who use this strategy fall into? How do you create your newsletter so it's fun and profitable?

These are the five key elements to producing that all important newsletter:

- objective and strategy
- content
- format
- frequency
- evolution.

I'll cover these five elements in brief for you now.

Objective and strategy

Firstly, you need to be crystal clear as to how your newsletter fits into the overall picture of your business. You must know what the objective of your newsletter is and whether it falls in line with your marketing strategy. Your newsletter must reflect your strategy in its pages.

Your objective could be to be seen as an expert or authority in your field, to be perceived as a pioneer or leader, i.e. someone who identifies trends or has new cutting-edge information which helps businesses to grow, regionally or nationally. Or, perhaps, you want to be regarded as the most expensive in your market, while at the same time a provider of value for money and a superb service. Whatever your objective, it must be clear.

Never assume that your customers will know all about the different services or products you have as, more often than not, they won't. Your newsletter can be used as a way to educate the reader.

Content

What's included in your newsletter is more important than what it looks like – a stylish newsletter won't always win your reader if the content is poor. So, put a great deal of thought into what you're going to include.

Think about what would add value, answer questions that are posed frequently, inform customers on how to get the most out of your business, or generally improve their lives. Give them insights into trends.

Format

Here are a few considerations when you start to format your newsletter. Firstly, what should your newsletter look and feel like? Will you opt for a full colour, 12-page extravaganza? Or a simple three- or four-page newsletter printed on your laser printer?

Whatever you decide, it must fit in with the image you want portray to your market. If you're selling a high-priced product, then a home-printed version may not be the best way to go. It'll give out the wrong impression and you don't want to send out the wrong message.

If your customers are more upmarket, and this is where you want to focus your attention, then you should opt for a professionally designed newsletter.

Frequency

The power of a newsletter is in the regularity and the frequency.

As a minimum, a newsletter should go out every three months. Any longer than that and the reader might well think that you've given up and abandoned them.

How often you send out your newsletter will depend on the nature of your business.

For business-to-business applications, a monthly communication is generally good, for customer-focused newsletters, where the value of the sale is lower, bi-monthly or quarterly newsletters should be the right frequency.

You'll find plenty of services on the internet, who'll be able to write the content for your newsletter at relatively little cost, e.g. iWrite.com, Elance.com, Guru.com, Freelancer.com and many others.

Evolution

Let's explore how your newsletter could develop.

I once worked for an international consulting firm and one of its clients was a fitness centre. Their newsletter started life with just a few pages and eventually turned into a 48-page colour magazine. I'm not suggesting yours should go the same way, but do look at how it could evolve.

You could start with just a few articles focused on one subject, either written by you or a freelancer, or several which are on related but different subjects.

If you commission others to write your newsletters, it takes the pressure off you.

However there is a risk. Your newsletter may lose a bit of impact if it starts to become a little too general. Extending it to different topics of interest might degrade your position in the market.

Host beneficiary opportunities

Many small business owners have lots of opportunities to leverage the goodwill and custom from a non-competing business, but there are very few who are aware of this simple, yet powerful, marketing approach.

So what is a 'host beneficiary' or, as it's also known, 'host parasite' relationship. (I prefer the former term.)

Here's an example of how this idea works and a glimpse as to how you can get it to work in your business.

Let's say there is a small restaurant owner who is pretty marketing savvy. She comes up with an idea to approach respected car dealers in her town and form a host beneficiary relationship. She puts forward a plan to the car dealers, which will enable them to put a compelling offer of a free three-course meal in front of their past customers, at relatively low cost to themselves.

All their past customers have to do is walk in to their dealerships and test drive one of their new models. After the test drive the prospective customer gets a VIP voucher which they can redeem at the restaurant. After the prospects have enjoyed their wonderful meal, taken in the atmosphere and generally had a good time, the restaurant owner sends a bill to the dealers for, say, £20, which represents a contribution towards the cost of the meal.

It's a wonderful opportunity for the dealers, as they're getting prospects who have identified themselves as being in the market for a new car and they have done it at a cost of £20 per prospect, rather than spending far more on other advertising methods. In effect, the acquisition cost would be far, far lower using this marketing approach.

Rather than the dealers going for a hard-sell, they now have a nice, non-pushy approach when contacting their past customers, which will generate goodwill, along with increasing showroom traffic.

The more people they have in their showroom, the more chances they have to sell more cars: a simple numbers game.

Nothing like a WIN/WIN

You're wondering what the reward would be for our restaurant owner. Well, even though she is practically giving away the meal, she has the chance to convert some of those past car dealer customers into her customers. Therein lies the WIN/WIN.

Here is an example of a letter a car dealer could have sent to their customers:

Hello Mr Sealey,

I feel just a bit awkward.

You see, in my office my team refer to you as a 'VIP Customer'... yet ...

I was talking with one of my sales team members and we both said we've not really had the opportunity to do anything 'VIP-ish' for you since you purchased your car from us back in September.

I thought straightaway, let me make up for that...

Firstly, we felt ANY VIP customer of ours should be invited to experience the buzz of test driving the new Zeppa.

When I say buzz, you have to be in the car to really appreciate that statement.

Secondly, I really do feel I'd be doing you a disservice if I didn't tell you about this and give you the opportunity to at least FEEL that sensational buzz.

I'd like to invite you to drop in (I'll be calling you in the next few days to arrange a suitable time) and get behind the wheel of this lovely car...

As you're a VIP, I want to make your visit to the dealership really special. So when you do come in, I'd like to buy you a dinner for two, on us, at one of my very favourite restaurants in town...

It's a delightful little establishment called Best Restaurant on London Road.

Now let's say that the dealer sent out that letter to 1500 past customers: 5% took them up on the offer and 12% of those bought the new Zeppa. That's 9 new cars sold and 9 people who are delighted with their new car.

Let alone the 75 past customers who went back to the dealer, had a great experience with a business who thought enough of them to invite them along. Plus the 1,425 other past customers, who may now be interested in buying again at some time.

You can see how a host beneficiary relationship can give you access to customers of a non-competing business at little cost to you. Think about how you could put this marketing tactic to work for you.

Give your customers a magic moment

We all like pleasant surprises. More so, customers who buy from a supplier and all they get, in the way of a communication, is a letter asking them to buy something else. What can you do that would create advocacy in your customers and to differentiate yourself from others who supply them?

Give them a magic moment.

What do I mean by a 'magic moment'? It's something they'll love, which comes out of the blue.

I once worked with a UK design agency. It was a small creative agency, but had some really good clients. They called me, after sitting in on one of my seminars, and asked if I could help them.

They wanted their clients to see them differently from other suppliers. So we went about exploring ways they could do that. We then settled on an idea, which was simple, low-cost and would have an impact on decision-makers in the businesses they served.

We located local pizza takeaways and at lunchtime we ordered pizzas to be delivered to the clients at work. We attached a message simply saying, 'We bet you must be hungry, just about now' with their name at the bottom of the note.

The result? It went down a storm.

The agency was talked about for weeks; every time they called up, people would refer to them as the design pizza guys. It created a buzz and had the desired effect. They were seen as different and they were remembered.

Another magic moment I recall from my days as a consultant for an international consulting firm, was when one of our clients decided to have a 'Customer Appreciation' day.

When one of their customers called within that hour, they would be greeted with 'Congratulations, you're a winner! To say thank you for being a customer, we wanted to show our appreciation by buying you a hot-air balloon ride for two'.

This business used a variation of the host beneficiary tactic, so the balloon ride cost nothing, but the customer's perception was that it had been purchased for them. The balloon company got a flood of new potential customers on days that the balloon would be in the air anyway, so they didn't have to make any special arrangements.

Another example of a WIN/WIN. The result? Their clients would ring a little more regularly, just in case they were a winner. Word went round, people talked about it and even the local paper picked up the story and ran with it. An added bonus.

What magic moments could you put in place, within a system, so they definitely happen? Put them in the diary and let them just run; you'll be surprised what reactions you get.

Educating your customers

The amount of times I've heard business owners say, 'If only people knew about what we do and how we do it, I'm sure more would buy.'

They're right, if only more people were educated about what a business does, more of them would buy. What some small business owners don't realize is that there are ways you can educate prospects and turn those who are non-believers into fans.

Here are a couple of ideas to get you going.

Delivering superb customer service

It's really commonsense. A good guideline is to do what you would expect from a business that would delight you.

When someone orders a product, let them know that you're received their order and it's being processed. Give them regular updates on how far along their order is, and when they're likely to receive it.

Call them and let them know that their product is just moments away.

When delivering a service, do the same: let the client know when you'll be arriving and if you're late, have your service guarantee ready to be put into action. If you're late by more than 15 minutes, the service is on you.

Handling complaints

If there is a complaint, go out of your way to put it right. Most, if not all, businesses would do this anyway. But you go WAY further. You actually have a customer-complaint strategy, where you delight customers with a great comeback.

You give them the product, all depending on the value of course, for free. Or, offer something extra for free by way of an apology. Having a great comeback after a complaint will increase the likelihood that the same customer will buy from you again by up to 7,500%. The customer may also talk to others about what you did to put things right.

So it's worth having a strategy in place.

After your customer receives your product or service, follow up to ensure it was as expected and to reassure them that your door is always open if there are any issues. Yes, all commonsense, but you'd be surprised how rare commonsense can be when it comes to delivering customer service.

Those are just a few ideas, and perhaps you do some already. But you have to be consistent. Always get feedback from customers and they'll help you to identify weaknesses in your service so you can close those gaps and deliver brilliantly every single time. Ask your customers regularly about your service: what they liked and what they didn't. Check on the percentage of deliveries that arrived on time and how many didn't. Monitor the number of complaints you have received and what was done about them. How many customers were lost as a result of not delivering, and how many were saved as a result of a great comeback.

Measure your service levels: the more you know what's happening, the easier it will be to put right any issues.

Setting up a marketing back-end

By focusing on reducing the number of customers you lose, known as attrition, you impact on the amount of sales and profits you earn.

In keeping more customers, you are essentially giving yourself a grand opportunity to sell products or services at the 'back-end' and make your business more profitable.

But what are 'back-end' sales?

As the term suggests, it's selling your customers more products and services after their initial purchase.

Businesses everywhere will put a lot of time and effort into acquiring customers, as they feel that's the most effective way to build a good client database to nurture over time. And they are right.

However, the problem lies in the cost of acquiring those customers in the first place.

A small business may pay for an advert in a magazine costing, for example, £1,000, which is supposedly targeting their ideal prospects. That advert produces, let's say, just ten sales.

So the up-front cost of acquisition for each of the ten new sales is £100. Depending on the margin of what's being sold, that acquisition cost may surpass the profit on the sale. If the small business owner's focus was profit at the front-end, then they would be well-advised to ditch this method, because they're just not earning anything from the sales. They're working hard at the front-end and not reaping anything at the back-end.

However, if this same business owner has a strategy for turning front-end, low-margin sales into highly profitable back-end long term profits, then they'll be on their way to achieving a bumper harvest from every customer they bring onboard.

They understand that it's going to be the ongoing sales from those ten customers, which will really count over the next couple of years.

Our marketing savvy small business owner won't leave this to chance. They'll put in place an ongoing programme which will promote to these newly-won customers. It'll present to them a series of back-end products and services that they can buy. As a result of having a long-term, consistent programme, the business owner will foster loyalty and give those customers a sense of being cared for and that their business is appreciated.

Additionally, they'll ensure that they regularly inform customers of topics of interest and so on... thus building a relationship which will last.

For your business to be successful in any economic landscape, having a two-step approach, as in the example above, will set you on your way to being profitable. In a way, it'll be like writing yourself a blank cheque.

Summary

There are many ways to harvest your crop. And the methods I've outlined represent a fraction of what you could do. But what I've shared should give you ideas about what you can do now, which will have an impact of the quality and number of customers you attract.

Acquiring customers is important, it's the lifeblood of any enterprise, but keeping them is just as vital. You need to split your time between winning and retaining customers to remain in business. Yet many small businesses have fallen at this hurdle.

Your focus should be looking at ways to increase sales after an initial purchase, to nurture and follow up as often as possible, along with building lasting relationships, which will encourage customers to come back and buy often.

Fact-check (answers at the back)

1. Should there be something in place to welcome a new customer to your business?
   a) There is no need for that ❏
   b) Yes, but only when they have been with me for six months ❏
   c) Not necessarily, it really depends on the customer ❏
   d) Yes absolutely, as it reinforces the reason why they chose your business ❏

2. Which of the following is an important consideration when creating a newsletter?
   a) The adverts ❏
   b) Making sure it goes out ad hoc ❏
   c) The content ❏
   d) Ignoring the objective and strategy ❏

3. Is it a good idea to have an objective and strategy to your newsletter?
   a) Yes ❏
   b) No ❏
   c) Sometimes ❏
   d) Only halfway through the first year ❏

4. What businesses can you approach with a host beneficiary opportunity?
   a) Should be a business with totally different customer profiles ❏
   b) Any business with a similar customer base ❏
   c) You should never approach a business with this marketing tactic ❏
   d) Only businesses in your sector ❏

5. What is meant by a customer 'magic moment'?
   a) Giving your customer something they'll love, out of the blue ❏
   b) Sending your invoice late ❏
   c) Contacting your customer when they request it ❏
   d) Delivering what the customer has asked for ❏

6. Is handling customer complaints a method of educating your customers?
   a) No ❏
   b) Possibly ❏
   c) Rarely ❏
   d) Yes ❏

7. In the section on delivering superb customer service, which of the following is an example used?
   a) Not contacting the customer with details of when their purchase is likely to arrive ❏
   b) Delivering the incorrect purchase ❏
   c) Making them feel like an annoyance when they call ❏
   d) If you're late by 15 minutes the service is on you ❏

8. When a customer receives a great comeback from a complaint, by how much do you increase the likelihood they'll use you again?
   a) 7,500% ❏
   b) 50% ❏
   c) 75% ❏
   d) 10% ❏

9. What are 'back-end' sales?
a) Selling your products out of the back door ❏
b) Having products and services to sell to customers after their initial purchase ❏
c) Only selling your lowest-priced item to customers ❏
d) Using telemarketers to sell your products ❏

10. What is meant by 'acquisition cost'?
a) The money customers pay for your products or services ❏
b) How much you pay your staff ❏
c) The cost of acquiring new stock ❏
d) How much it costs you to win a customer ❏

FRIDAY

Growing new crops

With yesterday's work you looked at welcoming customers to your business, delivering service and putting in place methods to keep your customers buying through your 'back-end' products or services. Serving your existing customers is a very profitable strategy to have in place, but every business needs an influx of new customers to maintain a steady flow of sales.

Today we'll look at some of the additional marketing tactics you can use to attract these new customers. Some of what you're about to learn you may be using already, in some shape or form. If not, they'll be a welcome addition to your marketing arsenal.

As I mentioned on Monday, you need to have multiple marketing channels to give your business the widest possible reach. Having different marketing tactics designed to win new customers, or to grow new crops, is essential.

Should one tactic not work as well as expected, you have others picking up the slack and generating sales for you. For a small business, having the reassurance of a system in place that generates business, almost automatically, is a comforting thing.

Running a small enterprise is stressful at the best of times, so having tactics in place to attract new customers relieves some of that stress and makes the whole experience more enjoyable. Yes, sales and profits are important. But being happy with what you're doing as well is just as important.

Let's get underway and start growing new crops...

Having referrals to build your business

There is something that most, if not all, businesses know, which is that referrals can be one of the most effective ways to get new customers.

When someone contacts you as a result of one of your existing customers recommending you, they are virtually ready to buy. It's the referral that tends to give you the lion's share of the business you get. And it far outstrips other methods of attracting the prized, ready-to-buy customer.

But yet, with all that said, many small business owners neglect to put in a place a system which generates referrals, as and when they need new business. They leave it in the lap of the gods, assuming that referrals will come through the door.

How much does it cost to get referrals? Nothing, they're free. Furthermore, they come from credible sources – often loyal customers.

The referral system

There is a difference between getting new customers through word of mouth and getting them via a referral system.

With the former, those customers arrive at your business in a haphazard way. Whereas a referral system gives you more control; it's like a tap that you can turn on and off as and when you need new business.

Let me share with you some ideas to consider when you are looking at getting referrals in your business. These may sound obvious and simple. You tend to find the best ways are the simplest.

1 Ask

Now that sounds simple enough and it is. All you have to do is ask customers to recommend you and then follow up with those that you've asked. With this easy and obvious way of getting referrals, why don't more business owners use it?

Many feel awkward and uncomfortable. If that's the case and asking for referrals still fills you with dread, then do it using a postcard or a letter.

You can position your request more as an after-thought and so it seems a lot less pushy to those who receive it.

2 Thank those who refer

The fact that someone gives you a referral is testimony to the quality of your offering or you wouldn't get recommendations.

So, when someone does refer others to you, you should thank them for the referral and keep them informed as to what has happened with the new customer. By thanking people, you encourage them to make more referrals.

3 Give referrals

Your customers aren't the only ones who can refer others to you. Your suppliers, your accountant, solicitor, others in business that you know: all these people can refer customers your way.

Therefore, a great way to have lots of referrals knocking on your door is to give them out. When you give something away or help someone, they feel obliged to return the favour. You can imagine how well that works when it comes to referrals.

4 Ask the right people

Now you may be wondering what is meant by asking the 'right' people. If you were to categorize your customer base as follows:

● A = Ardent fans
● B = Bulk of your database, neither As nor Cs
● C = You would rather be without them

A group of customers you would rather not ask are your Cs. These are the customers who would beat you down on price and are never satisfied; they take up 80% of your time but only give you 20% of your profits.

These are the customers you don't ask. You would only attract similar customers to your business, which could turn out to be a headache for you.

Your A and B clients are the ones to approach for referrals. They will interact with similar people.

5 Referrals at the right time

Just because someone doesn't buy from you the first time round, doesn't mean you can't approach them for a referral.

Your offering may be just right but the timing, for whatever reason, is wrong. If they believe you have a good solution, then they shouldn't have any problem with referring others.

Furthermore, you don't have to wait until you've built a relationship with people before you ask for a referral, you can do so as soon as they've bought from you. This is a time when they are excited by what they've purchased and they are at their most expectant.

6 Following up

There is one area of referrals that many businesses fall down on, and that's follow up.

Customers have taken the time and effort to extol the virtues of a business, and have shared with their closest friends, colleagues and business associates the benefits of using that business.

They give the business the contact details of those people they have spoken with and then the business does nothing. There is no follow up. So, ensure that you *always* follow up.

Special events

Hosting special events is a good way for prospective and current customers to engage with you, and to get a sense of receiving special treatment.

Sometimes, if your offering is for the consumer market, it can be a challenge to reach your customer either at work or at home. This is where events can be useful. Or, if you're having a problem moving dead stock, you can use a special event, marketing or education day to turn that dead stock into cash. People like attending events; they're a way to socialize, network and get to know suppliers. Plus, they may walk away with great deals.

Invitation only days

Another idea is to organize an 'invitation only' event.

For example, a bespoke, high-end furniture shop wants to run an invitation only open day to show existing customers and selected prospects how they craft high quality furniture in a traditional way.

The shop owner shows photographs of the furniture being made, in stages, and makes favourable comparisons with the furniture of other brands who, perhaps, use lower-quality materials.

Invitations are sent out to a relatively small number of people.

Closed door events

I don't see this method that often, and it's such a terrific way of moving dead stock, or anything else for that matter, quickly.

Small businesses can generate bundles of cash from their 'dead' or end-of-season stock, by running what is called a closed door event.

Now if you don't have a door to close, because of your type of offering, you will have to adapt this method to suit your business and call it something like an 'email day sale'. If you have premises, then a closed door event is more straightforward.

You could send out an email stating that you have stock you need to dispose of to make way for new lines from the companies who supply you.

The message could read 'We all make mistakes and I've made one... I've overstocked.'

The email will give the date and time of the sale and add that 'everything will go', to create the idea of scarcity. Include a line like 'It'll be first come, first served'. You could say that orders received by 2 p.m. will also receive an added privilege.

Telemarketing to win

Every time I speak with small business owners, and telemarketing or telesales comes into the conversation, there is always an air of dread. People aren't very keen on having to pick up a phone and market to people.

Research has indicated that the vast majority of people who receive telephone sales calls were annoyed by them.

So it's hardly surprising that many businesses don't like making them. But the telephone is still an excellent marketing and sales tool, whether it's for business-to-consumer or business-to-business.

Telemarketing is a relatively low cost way of contacting and engaging prospects and customers. The authors Bob Stone and John Wyman wrote a book in 1985, much of which is still relevant today, called *Successful Telemarketing: Opportunities and Techniques for Increasing Sales and Profits*. They coined the phrase 'Telemarketing Sales Continuum', in which they identified the different points in a sales process where the telephone could really be harnessed after a lead had been created.

One use of telemarketing in your business is simply to ring customers who are about to lapse on a subscription, membership or renewal of insurance. You've probably been on the receiving end of these types of calls yourself. You can make and save money with these types of communications.

Stand up and speak

Seminars, workshops, speaking to an audience or group of people, are great ways to get your message across, in person, to a number of people. This is more efficient than selling one to one, and trying to get a 100% conversion on every call.

So if you convert 10% of a room of 100 prospects, that's 10 prospects you've converted into customers with just one presentation.

When people turn up to a seminar or workshop to listen to an expert speaking on a topic, they have invested time and money to attend. Therefore, they are looking for a golden bullet, some kind of solution to a problem they may have.

By giving a rousing speech and letting them know, through the content you deliver, that you are a person who can solve their problem, you can turn a number of prospects into customers.

I've acquired the vast majority of my clients through this method of marketing. I often get a bumper harvest by this strategy alone.

That's the power of it.

Effective networking

Connecting with others to build, nurture and win new customers, or 'networking' as we all know it, has become an essential skill that small business owners have been focusing on for many years. It is a great way to prepare your ground.

Before I explore with you some of the tactical ways you can network effectively, let me share the following attributes I believe you need to have when looking to connect with others:

- to be purposeful
- to be passionate
- to be committed
- to be sincere
- to be an educator.

Network on purpose

You need to know why you're attending networking events and what, ideally, you would like to get out of them. As the term suggests, the event is to 'net-work' not 'net-social'.

I don't have enough spare time to attend all the events I'm invited to, so I have to be very selective. By getting a list of others attending, in advance, I can see who I would like to meet and start to build a relationship with.

Passion sells

You can see and feel the commitment in a person. If they're passionate about something, it'll come over in no uncertain terms. Enthusiasm is infectious, it rubs off on people. And the fact that you display passion about what you do tells others you must be worth listening to, at the least to find out what you're so passionate about.

Be committed to connecting

The fact that you turn up to many networking events, and that you're regularly seen by many other business owners, is a sign that you're committed to meeting and connecting with others.

By being that consummate networker you can be regarded as a centre of influence and business opportunities will seek you out, as opposed to the other way round. What you say, how you say it, the people you introduce to each other and the information you send to people you meet after events, all communicate your commitment.

Sincerity builds trust

There is nothing worse than speaking to someone who, you feel, isn't being genuine. All you want to do is get away from them as quickly as possible. The lack of sincerity may not be intentional; perhaps they've gone to an event with no purpose other than to sell. They've missed the whole idea of networking.

The more sincere you are, the more opportunities will come your way. People will be more inclined to open doors for you, if they trust you. I'm not sure who coined this phrase, but it's a very good one. 'All things being equal, people will do business with those people they know, like and trust.'

Understanding others

St Francis of Assisi, in his famous prayer to God, said 'Seek first to understand and then be understood'; this is the key to communicating effectively.

It's this principle you should be taking into EVERY networking event. It sits at the core of how we all do business, or it should. You need to be aware of the needs and wants of the businesses you're connecting with.

So, pay attention to details, listen intently, share comments, thoughts and resources, but, more importantly, make yourself available to people. If you've experienced any kind of sales training, you'll recall the old but true saying, 'You have two ears and one mouth and you should use them in that order'.

The obvious and not so obvious

There are a number of 'musts' when attending networking events.

Firstly, arrive early; this gives you the opportunity to introduce yourself to everyone who walks in. By the time everyone has arrived you will have met them all.

Secondly, dress appropriately. This doesn't mean 'suited and booted', but appropriate to the industry you're in. If a gardener you'd invited to look over your garden and give you a quote, walked up your pathway wearing a suit and carrying a briefcase, you'd think something was wrong with that picture. You have an expectation of what a gardener would dress like.

Thirdly, ensure that you have a plentiful supply of business cards. That's an obvious point, but you'd be surprised at how many people run out of them. Also, take postcards pre-printed with a simple message, such as 'It was great meeting you and thanks so much for sharing what you do. If I ever come across someone who's in the market for what you offer I'll certainly pass your details on.'

Another obvious point is to know what you want to say when asked what you do. People have a short attention span, so what you say has to be concise and benefit-oriented. If you can tell people what you do in 30 seconds or less, and they instantly understand the benefits, then that's great.

Call this your 30-second advert if you like. And it would go something like this:

> **You know how** *many companies who need to improve their performance are too busy fire-fighting,* **which means that** *they steadily become less competitive, until one day they find they have no customers?*
>
> **Well what I do is** *take them through a business success process,* **which means that** *they find themselves in a stronger position to get and keep more clients, and better clients, than ever before. And they have a business that's a rejuvenated, high-performance money machine.*

Some people have said that this is an outmoded method, but it still works. The key thing is to mix it around every so often, so that you don't get bored repeating yourself, and those on the receiving end don't recognize the same old format.

Here's the format for you:

- **You know how** – *characterize a typical problem or behaviour*
- **which means that** – *state the poor consequences*
- **Well what I (or we) do is** – *characterize what it is that you do*
- **which means that** – *state the benefits*.

Bob Berg, an authority on networking and outstanding when it comes to fostering relationships through networking, came up with some questions to ask when in a networking situation.

He calls them 'Feel Good' questions. They are designed to connect you with people quickly, especially at a busy event where you want to work a room fast.

Thank you, Bob Berg, for these great questions:

- How did you get started in the xyz business?
- What do you enjoy most about your profession?
- What separates your company from your competition?
- What advice would you give someone just starting in the xyz business?
- What one thing would you do with your business if you knew you couldn't fail?
- What significant changes have you seen take place in your profession through the years?
- What do you see as the coming trends in the xyz business?
- Describe the strangest or funniest incident you've experienced in your business.
- What ways have you found to be the most effective for promoting your business?
- What one sentence would you like people to use in describing the way you do business?

This is the ONE key question that'll separate you from the others in the room:

- How will I know if someone I'm talking to would be a good prospect for you?

Now I've used all of these questions at various times, but that last one tells me, and will tell you, exactly what that business is looking for.

To this day, I haven't been asked that question by anyone I've networked with. And I suspect that, when I've asked that question, it's the first time the person has been asked it at an event. Instantly I'm separated from others in the room, but more importantly I'm remembered.

Networking is an art and a skill you can develop. Done correctly, it can be a MAJOR contributor for you achieving a BUMPER harvest.

Exhibition or trade shows

Trade shows have been around since the earliest days of civilization; they were called marketplaces or bazaars. And they took pride of place in small towns and cities around the world. Vendors from all over the region would flock together to sell their wares to local people and businesses.

Today, trade shows have grown into international events with thousands of companies selling their products and services, and using the most advanced techniques available today.

If you exhibit, or intend to, at trade shows, fairs or exhibitions, the ideas I'm about to share with you will help you to get the most out of any event you attend.

Look the part

Create the right impression by looking polished, sharp and professional. Unless your business is leisure-orientated, wear business-like dress, but ensure it's comfortable. You'll be wearing it all day.

If you haven't got one already get a name tag with your company logo and your Unique Selling Proposition statement on it.

Get plenty of rest and pace yourself throughout the exhibition. You'll need a break or two so ensure that you schedule those in.

Hosting your stand

- Send invites to the press, past customers, existing customers and prospects to visit you at the show.
- Send out a map for those customers you're inviting prior to the exhibition and show your location. Make it easy for them.
- If you have the space, provide refreshments at your stand.
- Again, if you have the space, include some comfortable seating.
- Ensure that the signage you use includes (along with your company name) the benefit that is derived from using your product or service.
- Use an offer to entice people to come to your stand and a prize draw as a way to collect business cards. They are old, but trusted techniques.

- Try not to leave your stand unattended. Visitors may walk away or pass your stand if you're not there; they perceive it as a lack of interest in providing information. When you leave on a break ensure you have cover.

Be approachable

Your visitors will want face-to-face contact. Eighty-five per cent of communication is non-verbal, so use non-verbal cues to show you have genuine interest in talking with them. Smile, make eye contact and extend your hand. Match the handshake of the visitor: people like those who are just like them. This is a very quick way to establish rapport.

Listen

I mentioned this in the networking section and it's a key skill to have. Once you've got the attention of your visitor, listen carefully to their needs and interests. Find out what they want by asking open questions.

Know your stuff

This may sound obvious, but you'd be surprised at how many exhibitions and trade shows I've been to where the staff manning the stands didn't have all the relevant knowledge to deal with enquiries.

On the odd occasion there will be a question which you'll be unable to answer. Offer to get the answer(s) for the enquirer and get their details.

Keep records of visitors

Devise a simple record card which captures the details of your visitors:

- name
- position
- company name
- telephone
- email
- website address.

Also record any interests and needs they had. You'll be able to use this information in your follow up.

Identify and disqualify

Time can be wasted with visitors who are just not interested in what you do. You need to identify them early by asking some key questions – while you're talking to someone who will not make a good prospect, your ideal customer may well be standing behind them ready to leave.

When asked 'What do you do?', this is where your 30-second advert comes in. Refer back to the networking section of today to refresh your memory. You want to get to the heart of the matter quickly, so people can spend more time with you and you can find out more about them.

Follow up

You've invested time and money in this exhibition. Maximize on the whole event by following up. I've been to exhibitions in the past, and to this day I still haven't received a follow up from ANY of the companies I spoke to. Following up is VITAL!

Those are just a few key tips, and really are the commonsense approaches you should have when going to any exhibition or show. There are others, of course, but these will get you moving in the right direction.

Sponsorship to win new customers

If done well, being a sponsor can bring a great deal of exposure, brand your business and attract customers.

However, like everything we've discussed, it has to be part of your overall strategy. I'm going to walk you through some ideas that will get you thinking about this marketing option. After you've read through this, you'll be able to decide whether or not sponsorship is a viable marketing option for you.

To clarify: sponsorship is the support, financial or otherwise, of a live event, media and media broadcast, cause, sporting club, trade show, person or group. In fact you can sponsor any activity. Some small businesses confuse sponsorship with advertising. The two are different. You can see an immediate result with advertising, done well that is.

There are as many sponsorship opportunities as there are small businesses to take advantage of them; there's no need to look towards the big, grand opportunities, which most small business just can't afford. Instead seek out smaller and more cost-effective opportunities, which will target your marketing more effectively.

Sponsorship enables you to enhance an image you want to portray, and it can shape the attitude that people have, or will have, towards you. It can also give you the opportunity to showcase products and services, and can drive sales up.

With any sponsorship approach you have to be clear about who you want to target. Obvious I know. But a surprising number of companies have gone into a sponsorship opportunity and missed the mark totally. That isn't a mistake you should make.

When reaching out with sponsorship you want to:

1 Define your target market and be clear about the type of message you want to communicate. Is it to change your market's perceptions? Or is it about modifying their behaviour in some way?
2 Be realistic when it comes to the results you want. You can get a little too enthusiastic, if there is such a thing, and overestimate and generalize your market. And you'll want to remember that not everyone will want what you offer.

The more research you do to ascertain what your market wants and needs, and what motivates them, the better placed you'll be to find the ideal sponsorship opportunity.

You should seek sponsorship opportunities that will:

● help to build your database with highly qualified leads
● enhance your influence at networking events
● increase loyalty

- increase the amount of sales you get
- ramp up the traffic to your website
- build on relationships.

Finally, here are a few tips, which will keep you on track if this is your first foray into sponsorship:

1 Avoid getting caught up in all the buzz and attention that'll come your way through being a sponsor. You'll spend a large amount of time dealing with stuff which is mainly cosmetic in nature.
2 Don't be tempted to go for too big a sponsorship opportunity. As I mentioned earlier, you may be better off targeting smaller, niche areas.
3 Focus on what you want to achieve from using this strategy, to avoid waste. Don't get side-tracked with other options which could be part of any sponsorship deal.
4 Always look for alternatives to giving cash; there are ways that you can have an 'in-kind' contribution for sponsorship.

Summary

As you now know, there are many things you have to take into account when looking to achieve a bumper harvest. Referrals can give you a good number of new ready-to-buy customers are a great source of sales.

If you want an approach that would give your prospects and customers personal interaction with you, then hosting special events can work very well. They give you a number of opportunities to educate and inform your customer base, and you can sell to more than one person at a time.

Don't underestimate the power of networking. It helps you to establish yourself as an expert in your field and can open up new business opportunities.

Attending exhibitions and using sponsorship are good ways to raise your profile and get your message across to a wider audience.

SUNDAY
MONDAY
TUESDAY
WEDNESDAY
THURSDAY
FRIDAY
SATURDAY

Fact-check (answers at the back)

1. How many things do you need to consider when trying to get referrals?
   - a) 6 ❑
   - b) 5 ❑
   - c) 4 ❑
   - d) 3 ❑

2. Which categories of clients should you approach for referrals?
   - a) Only approach group A – your most loyal customers ❑
   - b) Only approach group B – the majority of your customers ❑
   - c) Only approach group C – difficult customers ❑
   - d) Approach both group A and group B, but avoid group C ❑

3. Which of the following are three examples of how you can use special events?
   - a) Invite customers to a party, invite friends to a party, invite family to a party ❑
   - b) Education days, moving dead stock, networking ❑
   - c) Socialize with your competitors, meet local government officials, invite suppliers to pitch to you ❑
   - d) There are no examples of how to use special events? ❑

4. Which of the following is one way to use telemarketing?
   - a) Calling customers who are about to lapse ❑
   - b) Confirming product amounts with suppliers ❑
   - c) Calling to confirm arrival dates of supplies ❑
   - d) Dealing with customer complaints ❑

5. Which of the following is an effective alternative to your speaking alone at an event?
   - a) Send out a report about the topic ❑
   - b) Play a recording to the audience instead ❑
   - c) Don't have speeches at all ❑
   - d) Share the platform with non-competing businesses, who have a similar customer base ❑

6. By what percentage can a headline increase the spend and pulling power of your communication?
   - a) 10% ❑
   - b) 40% ❑
   - c) 80% ❑
   - d) 500% ❑

7. If you attend a trade-show, fair or exhibition, how many areas do you need to consider to help you get the most out of any event you attend?
   - a) 3 ❑
   - b) 6 ❑
   - c) 8 ❑
   - d) 10 ❑

8. Which of the following should you do when attending a trade fair or exhibition?
   - a) Keep records of visitors ❑
   - b) Be approachable ❑
   - c) Know your stuff ❑
   - d) All of the above ❑

9. What does sponsorship enable you to enhance?
a) Your position as the business owner ❏
b) The image you want to portray, and people's attitude towards your business ❏
c) The profile of your staff ❏
d) Your competitors' view of you ❏

10. What does networking enable you to do?
a) Have the computers in your office all linked up ❏
b) Sell to new prospects as soon as you walk in the door ❏
c) Socialize with others you don't know ❏
d) Build relationships, nurture and win new customers ❏

SATURDAY

Knowing how much your crops will yield

You now have ideas for a range of new marketing techniques for your business, to enable you to attract more new customers.

Of all the areas in marketing that are vital to a business's ongoing success, measuring and managing is the most important. As the saying goes 'What you can measure you can manage, what you don't measure you cannot manage'. Knowing what works and what doesn't will earn you more profits and save you time.

I heard this saying when I first started in the marketing profession: 'Half of all marketing works, you just don't know which half.' So, without measuring, you don't know what works. Today we'll walk through the sort of measuring and managing approaches you should consider.

Why measure and manage?

Some small businesses find measuring marketing approaches a bit of a challenge, because they don't know what to measure or how to measure it. Moreover, they don't realize what impact measuring marketing activities, on a regular basis, can have on their business.

When a business does grasp how effective measuring their activities can be, the rewards are huge. They begin to see where their marketing spend is best used, which means they can make smarter decisions, giving them more of an edge over the competition. Business owners can see, at a glance, where to continue funding activities and where to drop them. For example, take something like a simple display advertisement in a newspaper versus a classified advert. You can measure the number of responses from each and then see which gives you a better return on the money spent.

Once you know which method gives you the better results, you can then manage a ongoing campaign using the more effective method and drop the one which didn't perform as well. The information from simply measuring what's going on in a business is invaluable.

There is nothing more gratifying than being able to see, instantly, where you're heading, when you have systems in place to measure your activities. It makes the management of those activities a lot easier and more fun.

YEP – IT'S BEEN A GOOD YEAR... I THINK...?

Every tweak and change could spell an increase in profits and a pay rise for the owner. That's why you should measure and manage. It should be the cornerstone of your marketing efforts.

What can be measured?

I was sitting here thinking about what items I could list to give you an idea of what you can start measuring in your business, if you're not already. The list just went on and on.

I came to the conclusion that everything can be measured.

There will be areas which will give you an immediate indication whether or not a strategy is working, like direct mail marketing, or text message marketing. With others, you'll have to dig a little deeper to get the information you need.

Go through this final day and list which areas of your marketing you can measure. Then look at how you would manage the information which comes from the data you get.

Let me give you a straightforward example, using a direct mail piece.

- You've created three different versions of a sales letter with the headlines and copy focusing on your target market's fears, frustrations and/or needs.
- You have split your database into As, Bs and Cs (leaving the C type customers out of any mailing, as you don't want to attract more Cs).
- Then you mail out the three different versions to a cross-section of your A and B customers.
- Now you measure the result: which letter gave you the best response. This is called 'Split Testing'.
- Once you have the information you can test different aspects of the letter to get the best return on your investment, before you roll out the best-performing version to the rest of your list. For example, you could refine the following basic elements:
  - headline
  - subheading
  - body copy

- offer
- guarantee
- call to action

Your online marketing efforts are quicker and easier to measure, as the tools are readily available, for example, counting the number of visitors to your site, which pages they go to, etc.

You should measure as much as you possibly can; that way you'll gain intelligence about your marketing which will put you in an optimum position compared to your competitors.

For example, you could look at the effectiveness of your referral system. When used does the system generate a good number of referred clients, who buy? Compare it with other marketing approaches you employ.

You could also see how effective your press releases are in generating interest. When circulating press releases, you should include contact details of a specific staff member at the end, who can then monitor responses as a direct result of the press release.

Conversion rates

I did say you can measure everything, but there is one area that very few small businesses measure at all, or if they do it's pretty infrequent. And that's conversion rates.

I once asked a business owner what her inbound call conversion rate was like. When she immediately replied 'Fantastic', I was worried. I knew activities in other areas weren't being measured, so it was unlikely that inbound calls were being checked.

Over the following week, we measured what the actual rate was. To her dismay, her quoted 85% conversion was more like 23%.

Seventy-three per cent of people calling in for this company's products and services were walking away. The business owner's marketing attracted them, but her team's skills at converting were letting her down. It wasn't their fault, they just weren't trained correctly. The owner had thought that giving her staff a brief induction and putting them straight on the phones would suffice; after all, this was an amazing business with great products and services to boot.

There needed to be a way to reverse this and decrease the number of people leaving after making an initial enquiry. We set about achieving this and, at the end of only two weeks, the derisory 23% had jumped to an impressive 66%.

A telephone skills training programme was introduced: how to greet the caller, how to ask questions, and what information to get even before details were given about the product or service. These small improvements had a massive impact on sales, profits and, here was the key thing, morale.

Measuring the effectiveness of conversions

Once you have increased your conversion rates, you need to know how effective those conversions really are.

Earlier in the week we talked about finding your star performer and using them as a benchmark. Just as you would find the best sales presentation for everyone to use, you would also find the best converters and evaluate the process from enquiry to sale.

You'll need to measure at each stage of the sales process how effective it is: look at how many people fall out at stage one, stage two or stage five, whatever is appropriate for you. By finding the weak spots, you can do something about them to shore them up and achieve better results.

Positioning proposals

Another area which most businesses get involved with is sending out quotes. Now this will be the last time you hear use this term, 'quote'.

Whenever you send a prospect or customer a quote, what you're inadvertently saying is 'Go out and find a better price'. So change the word quote to 'proposal' (for example); anything but quote.

Using the word 'proposal' assumes that you've already won their custom, so how you position the information will be starkly different.

This is an area that small businesses can easily measure. You can judge the effectiveness of your proposals, with the change of wording, by keeping a record of any sales which come in as a direct result, compared with previous sales, or the number of sales when no proposal is sent. In addition, you can see whether conversions have increased.

Managing activities

If you have a small team of people and everyone gets involved in the day-to-day running of the business, it's important that you have a process for managing your marketing activities.

Without having something in place to keep a handle on what's going on with all your marketing activities, things can quickly spiral out of control.

So, keep a close eye on your spending, which marketing strategies are working and which aren't, and how effective each approach is. Managing this way will increase profits and reduce wastage.

Just having a simple procedure when using any marketing activity will enable you to save time, money and effort. Smaller businesses need to maximize every opportunity and having a procedure in place will help you mange things much more easily, giving you time to focus on other areas of your business.

One example here could be implementing a process, which is documented, whenever new enquiries come in. You select two people to share the duties of taking enquiries, they in turn move them up, after taking the essential details, to someone in your team who sells a product or service which meets the enquirer's needs, and they in turn hand over the sale to someone who would be responsible for delivery. A simple procedure, which is documented and which everyone knows, is easy to manage.

If you have a presence on any of the many social networking sites like Facebook, Twitter, LinkedIn or Google Plus, managing this on a daily basis can be a mammoth task.

But it does need to be managed, or you'll quickly lose the confidence of those trying to interact with you. Having a period of the working day where messages, posts or enquiries can be dealt with will pay off. It's a basic example, but having a routine procedure like this enables you to manage an otherwise very time-consuming task.

Take an analysis

Now you've decided which marketing approaches you'll be using and have planned out who you'll be approaching, why and what will motivate them to buy. You'll need to test, measure and manage the methods and strategies used.

What will separate you from your competition, and sustain your marketing efforts and your business, is your commitment to tracking everything: your sales approaches, partnerships, referrals, online activities... everything you do, and then looking at how all of that compares to your spend.

You will get to a point where you know exactly how much you spend marketing your business and, in most cases, that figure will be fixed. The aim is to get as good a return as possible, in the way of sales and profits, from the money you invest.

If you're tracking marketing activities, you'll be able to see any gaps or weak areas. Then you can make improvements to achieve greater results.

As a rule, for any of your marketing tactics, it is a good idea to have a checklist so you measure and manage everything, and to record the initial costs of implementing each tactic.

Use the best performing strategies as your benchmarks; everything else you do will be measured against them. If your new tweaks, amendments or changes outperform your benchmarks, make them your new benchmarks.

You'll have more control over your business as opposed to the business having control over you. Every month your business will get better and better. The compound effect of measuring and managing will put you in a position to, potentially, double the value of your business year on year. And every year your business becomes twice as good.

Summary

It's not enough just to plan and implement marketing activities, you also have to measure and manage them, to give you even better results and to maximize the return on your investment, be that in time or money.

You will see instantly whether to shelve an approach or to build on it. By evaluating the responses you get, you can predict sales and profits and, more interestingly, you can spot trends before anyone else does. That's your competitive edge. Without measuring and managing, you cannot get that sort of information. Is it any wonder that many small businesses and start-ups fail because they don't do something as simple as keeping an eye on what works and what doesn't?

Remember, you can measure anything and you should measure everything, particularly your conversion rates. Knowing the effectiveness of conversions can give you an early 'heads up' about the systems you have in place.

Analyse all the data you get and consider the results as pure gold, as it will be those results that will make you and your business successful.

SUNDAY
MONDAY
TUESDAY
WEDNESDAY
THURSDAY
FRIDAY
SATURDAY

Fact-check (answers at the back)

1. What is one of the important aspects to ensuring your business success?
   a) Opening 7 days a week ❏
   b) Having at least 10 members of staff ❏
   c) Measuring and managing what you do ❏
   d) Making sure that you advertise in trade magazines ❏

2. Which one of the following is a reason to measure and manage?
   a) To see how much in bonuses needs to be paid ❏
   b) So you are seen as a great leader of people ❏
   c) You always know when you are running out of stock ❏
   d) It enables you to make better-informed decisions ❏

3. What can be measured?
   a) Nothing ❏
   b) Only five things in any business ❏
   c) Sales only ❏
   d) Everything can be measured ❏

4. Which one of the following is a good example of measuring conversion rates?
   a) Inbound phone enquiries to sales ❏
   b) Converting a piece of equipment for another purpose ❏
   c) Changing your selling currency to another currency ❏
   d) How quickly you can convert a prospect to a customer ❏

5. Could you use 'split testing' to measure results?
   a) No ❏
   b) Yes ❏
   c) Maybe ❏
   d) What is 'split testing'? ❏

6. Can you use a star performer in your business to measure the effectiveness of conversions?
   a) No ❏
   b) Why would you want to measure conversions ❏
   c) Yes ❏
   d) Any one of the team can be used to measure the best conversion rate ❏

7. What term should you use in place of the word 'quote'?
   a) Keep the word 'quote' ❏
   b) Summary ❏
   c) Proposal ❏
   d) Presentation ❏

8. Is it important to measure each stage of the sales process?
   a) No ❏
   b) Yes ❏
   c) Occasionally ❏
   d) Only when new products are introduced ❏

9. Is it beneficial to have a benchmark of your best performing strategies?
a) Yes as any new tweaks, amendments or changes can be measured against the benchmark ❏
b) No, it's not really beneficial ❏
c) It can be at times, but not always ❏
d) I would only have a benchmark if sales were low ❏

10. What's the advantage to analysing your marketing results?
a) You can see which methods work and which don't, and what strategy is giving you the best results ❏
b) You know how much money you should leave in your account ❏
c) It gives you peace of mind ❏
d) You shouldn't analyse the information, as you have better things to do ❏

7 × 7

1 Seven key ideas

- Capture and use your testimonials: All businesses get them from time to time. Go to your customers and get testimonials from them. Then use them in all of your marketing communications, to give social proof.
- Ethical bribes: Motivate people to take action with good offers. Create an offer so good it makes it difficult for customers to say no.
- Follow-up calls: Every time a customer purchases from you, follow up with them to make sure they are happy. It's a great service approach and also gives you another opportunity to sell them something else, or at the very least to gain a referral.
- Always send out press releases: There is always a lot happening in a business that the market doesn't always get to hear about it. So every time something happens – like moving offices, updating your website, you've won an award – create a press release. You just never know, the media might pick it up.
- Capture customers' mobile numbers: One low-cost way to increase sales is SMS text message marketing. Once a new customer buys from you, get permission to send them messages via SMS. You could send offers, promotions, or just educational texts. It's low cost and you can reach a large number of people instantly.
- Give customers magic moments: There is nothing like a pleasant surprise. You can create these surprises – these 'magic moments' – for your customers. They will remember you forever if you give them something they never expected.
- Reduce your commercial exposure: Make sure you have more than one contact in any business that is a customer. Ensure you have the details of the decision makers and influencers. Then create a communications calendar to

keep in contact with all those on the list. That way should one leave, you still have a relationship with others in the business who can say 'no' or 'yes' to you.

2 Seven best resources

- www.marketingsherpa.com – MarketingSherpa is a research institute specializing in tracking what works in all aspects of marketing
- www.druckerinstitute.com – Hailed by BusinessWeek as 'the man who invented management', Drucker has directly influenced a massive number of business leaders from all industries. This is a wonderful resource to get an insight into the challenges you'll face in the future.
- www.paloalto.com – Sales and Marketing Pro is the UK's leading sales and marketing planning software. Create your sales plan to help you sell like a pro and add punch to your marketing plan.
- www.strategicprofits.com – Provides a proven system that allows smart, but overwhelmed, business owners to quickly consolidate profitability, eliminate wasted effort, and put the best possible version of their business on autopilot.
- www.mobilecommercedaily.com – This is a wonderful resource for businesses to check out what's at the forefront of mobile commerce and retail. There is up-to-date news, as it happens, and a wealth of ideas that business owners can explore.
- www.trello.com – Infinitely flexible, incredibly easy to use, great mobile apps – and it's free. Trello keeps track of everything, from the big picture to the minute details.
- www.freebizplansoftware.com – Free marketing planning software and books to download for small business owners and entrepreneurs.

3 Seven great companies

- Simply Business (online insurance, London) is the UK's largest online business insurance broker. The company has been featured in The Sunday Times Tech Track 100 four times and in 2015 won The Sunday Times 100 Best Companies to Work For. It's an innovative and forward-thinking business, which spots opportunities and runs with them.

- IKEA (office and home furnishers, global) is a group of companies that spans many countries around the world. It is famed for its designs and ready-to-assemble furniture range. Up until January 2008, it was the world's largest furniture retailer and between 2007–8 its website attracted over 470 million visitors. A great example of a simple business idea being marketed well.

- Reliance Industries Limited (diversified group of manufacturing companies, India) is, by market capitalization, the second-largest publicly traded company in India. It owns businesses engaged in energy, petrochemicals, textiles, natural resources, retail and telecommunications. As India becomes an ever-increasing business super-power, this is a business to watch. It's another great example of a business leader who spots opportunities and turns them into something very interesting and profitable.

- Sinopec (successful state-run business, China) may seem like an odd entry to the 'seven great companies' list, especially with it being state owned. However it is a major petroleum and chemicals player on the global scene. Back in 2011, it was ranked fifth in sales in Forbes Global 2000 (not an easy feat) and in 2009, it was ranked ninth by Fortune Global 500, which in effect made it the first Chinese corporation to make the top ten. It's been going from strength to strength and doesn't look like slowing down any time soon. A very good example of when a business gets its teeth into a market and starts to dominate it.

- Virgin (multi-discipline business, UK) is a great example of a business that really utilizes its brand. It has been carefully crafted and nurtured, to a point that nearly all over the globe the Virgin logo, and what it stands for, is recognized.

- WestJet (international airline, Canada) is a Canadian airline that provides scheduled and charter air services to many destinations in Canada, the United States, Europe, Mexico, Central America and the Caribbean. Founded in the late 1990s, in tough economic conditions, it is now the second largest Canadian air carrier, only behind Air Canada. It's doing a great job of transporting 45,000 passengers daily and has a daily average of 425 flights. The airline business is a tough business and these guys have survived difficult times and come out the other side. An example of being committed to an idea and following through

- Google (Internet, USA) – what can be said about this company that hasn't already been said? It's just a monster of company, with innovative thinkers who test and measure everything, and who aren't afraid to let go of ideas that aren't working and to do it quickly. It is this approach of doing business that has led them to being a number one world business.

4 Seven inspiring people

- Peter Drucker – An Austrian-born American management consultant, educator, and author, whose writings contributed to the philosophical and practical foundations of the modern business corporation.
- Jay Abraham – An American business executive, conference speaker, and author. He is known for his work in developing strategies for direct-response marketing in the 1970s. In 2000, Forbes listed him as one of the top five executive coaches in the US.
- Seth Godin – An American author, entrepreneur, marketer, and public speaker. One of America's foremost marketing experts.
- Earl Nightingale – American radio personality, writer, respected speaker and author, dealing mostly with the subjects of human character development, motivation, excellence and meaningful existence; the so-called 'Dean of Personal Development'.
- Alan Sugar – An English business magnate, media personality, and political advisor.
- Dan Kennedy – Is one of the highest paid, most in-demand direct marketing consultants in America today.
- Jack Ma – With the biggest IPO in history under his belt, Alibaba founder and chairman Jack Ma is now the richest person in China.

5 Seven great quotes

- 'If you don't know where you're going, all roads lead there.' Laurence Eubank
- 'Doing the right thing is more important than doing the thing right.' Peter Drucker
- 'The key to all life is value. Value is not what you get, it's what you give.' Jay Abraham
- 'You are surrounded by simple, obvious solutions that can dramatically increase your income, power, influence and success. The problem is, you just don't see them.' Jay Abraham
- 'The cost of being wrong is less than the cost of doing nothing.' Seth Godin
- 'Unless a product becomes outmoded, a great campaign will not wear itself out.' Rosser Reeves
- 'The best ideas come as jokes. Make your thinking as funny as possible.' David Ogilvy

6 Seven things to do today

- Categorize your customer base As, Bs and Cs. The A customers will be the ones that give you the highest profit and are a dream to deal with. Your C clients are the ones that moan and groan. The revenue they give doesn't justify the time you spend on them. Your Bs are neither As nor Cs but have the potential to become really good customers. Put together a plan to contact your As and Bs every 90 days or less.
- Speak with your top customers and ask them to refer others like them to you. Create a referral pack with good valuable information inside, that will encourage those customers to refer.
- Monitor the traffic to your website. Find out where this traffic is coming from and put together marketing approaches to get even more people to your website.
- List out your top three marketing approaches and look at ways to increase each by just 10 per cent.
- Check your website on a mobile device. If your website isn't mobile friendly then add that to your tasks of things to get done. More of your customers have gone mobile and they demand that websites are mobile compatible.

- Get five of your very best testimonials and add them all to your social media accounts.
- Post one great idea your market can use to make or save money.

7 Seven trends for tomorrow

- Mobile is going to become the centrepiece of marketing for business. With smartphones, tablets and wearable devices all building up a head of steam, businesses will need to embrace these technologies and look at ways to build more personalized relationships with their customers.
- Businesses which are transparent will dictate brand–customer relationships. The marketplace is becoming more demanding and in the months and years ahead, customer engagement will become so important, that those who fail to engage and be transparent about their operations will struggle.
- Good, valuable content will always top the charts. The amount of information now at customers' fingertips is massive. They will spend shorter time on information that doesn't give value. Ensure whatever content you put out provides huge amounts of value.
- Social media is the new online gold and social media platforms the new must-have real estate.
- Video has been big online for a few years, but it's set to become even bigger. Online video is gathering pace. Businesses small and large are now beginning to use more video promotions, such as trailers for their products and services. With this medium becoming much easier to stream on mobile, this will be a battleground for companies in the future.
- SMS text message marketing seems like it's been around longer than the internet. But it's still in its early stages. Some businesses still haven't jumped onto the band-wagon to leverage the opportunity of SMS marketing. This still has the potential to be extremely rewarding.
- Decision makers will get younger and many more will be female. As young adults leave university and decide against being employed but becoming the employer, businesses will need to look more at how they engage with and articulate their offerings along with the channels they use.

Answers to questions

Sunday: 1c; 2d; 3b; 4a; 5b; 6d; 7a; 8b; 9c; 10a

Monday: 1b; 2a; 3a; 4b; 5b; 6a; 7b; 8a; 9a; 10d

Tuesday: 1c; 2a; 3c; 4b; 5c; 6c; 7c; 8c; 9a; 10b

Wednesday: 1a; 2c; 3a; 4c; 5d; 6c; 7b; 8d; 9b; 10a

Thursday: 1d; 2c; 3a; 4b; 5a; 6d; 7d; 8a; 9b; 10d

Friday: 1a; 2d; 3b; 4a; 5d; 6c; 7c; 8d; 9b; 10d

Saturday: 1c; 2d; 3d; 4a; 5b; 6c; 7c; 8b; 9a; 10a